ROUTLEDGE LIBRARY EDITIONS: SOCIOLOGY OF EDUCATION

Volume 3

THE PAROCHIALISM OF THE PRESENT

THE PAROCHIALISM OF THE PRESENT

Contemporary issues in education

G. H. BANTOCK

Routledge
Taylor & Francis Group

LONDON AND NEW YORK

First published in 1981 by Routledge & Kegan Paul Ltd

This edition first published in 2017
by Routledge
2 Park Square, Milton Park, Abingdon, Oxon OX14 4RN

and by Routledge
711 Third Avenue, New York, NY 10017

Routledge is an imprint of the Taylor & Francis Group, an informa business

© 1981 G. H. Bantock

British Library Cataloguing in Publication Data
A catalogue record for this book is available from the British Library

ISBN: 978-0-415-78834-2 (Set)
ISBN: 978-1-315-20949-4 (Set) (ebk)
ISBN: 978-1-138-22027-0 (Volume 3) (hbk)
ISBN: 978-1-138-22028-7 (Volume 3) (pbk)
ISBN: 978-1-315-41337-2 (Volume 3) (ebk)

Publisher's Note
The publisher has gone to great lengths to ensure the quality of this reprint but points out that some imperfections in the original copies may be apparent.

Disclaimer
The publisher has made every effort to trace copyright holders and would welcome correspondence from those they have been unable to trace.

The parochialism of the present
Contemporary issues in education

G. H. Bantock

Routledge & Kegan Paul
London, Boston and Henley

First published in 1981
by Routledge & Kegan Paul Ltd
39 Store Street, London WC1E 7DD,
9 Park Street, Boston, Mass. 02108, USA and
Broadway House, Newtown Road,
Henley-on-Thames, Oxon RG9 1EN
Set in IBM Press Roman
and printed in Great Britain by
Biddles Ltd, Guildford, Surrey

British Library Cataloguing in Publication Data

Bantock, G.H.

The parochialism of the present.
— (Routledge education books)
1. Educational sociology
I. Title
370.19   LC191

ISBN 0-7100-0746-9

The truth is, that the knowledge of external nature, and of the sciences which that knowledge requires or includes, is not the great or the frequent business of the human mind. Whether we provide for action or conversation, whether we wish to be useful or pleasing, the first requisite is the religious and moral knowledge of right and wrong; the next is an acquaintance with the history of mankind, and with those examples which may be said to embody truth, and prove by events the reasonableness of opinions. Prudence and justice are virtues, and excellencies, of all times, and of all places; we are perpetually moralists, but we are geometricians only by chance. Our intercourse with intellectual nature is necessary; our speculations upon matter are voluntary, and at leisure. Physical knowledge is of such rare emergence, that one man may know another half his life without being able to estimate his skill in hydrostaticks or astronomy; but his moral and prudential character immediately appears.

Those authors, therefore, are to be read at schools that supply most axioms of prudence, most principles of moral truth, and most materials for conversation; and these purposes are best served by poets, orators, and historians.

Dr Samuel Johnson, Lives of the Poets: John Milton

Contents

Acknowledgments

The following essays have appeared elsewhere, and I am grateful for permission to republish: 'Equality and education' in *Equality, Education and Society*, edited by Bryan Wilson and published by George Allen & Unwin, 1975; 'The parochialism of the present' in *Journal of Philosophy of Education*, 1979 (originally a lecture to the Philosophy of Education Society, London Division); 'The idea of a liberal education' in *Educational Review*, University of Birmingham, 1968-9; 'Discovery methods' in *Black Paper* II, published by the Critical Quarterly Society, 1969; 'Literature and the social sciences' in *Critical Quarterly*, 1975 (originally a paper given at the British Sociological Association Annual Conference, 1970); 'The death of Bazarov' in *Educational Philosophy and Theory*, published by the University of New South Wales, 1971; 'The arts in education' in a Conference Report on Aesthetic Education, published by the Derby Lonsdale College of Higher Education, 1979.

Most, however, have been revised especially for this volume. I am particularly grateful for the advice and interest of the editor of the series, Professor S.J. Eggleston. Needless to say, I remain responsible for the final outcome. My thanks, too, are due to my wife for preparing the index.

Introduction

The essays in this volume emanate from a very specific standpoint, one which it is important should be made explicit so that they can be read not only for their own sakes but also as illustrative of an approach to educational studies I believe to be fruitful. Briefly, it is time we recovered a sense of history; and within a resuscitated awareness of historic process, it is time we recalled a literature as a central energising force in the examination of our social and moral problems (among which, of course, education has a prominent place). Let me explain more fully the implications of these remarks in the context of educational studies, remarks concerning which these essays are offered as supportive evidence.

The whole orientation of educational studies in recent years has emphasised the immediate and the contemporary. Their progress — and that they can be said genuinely to have progressed goes some way to lighten the strictures I am about to pass — has been deeply influenced by the development of the social sciences. These sciences share with the natural sciences an anti-historical bent which marks their empiricism, their concern with observable and quantifiable aspects of behaviour in the here and now.[1] That this should be the case with psychology and sociology is, then, not surprising. But the movement earlier in the century which changed the orientation of philosophical studies, a movement which during the last twenty years has become a dominant voice in the philosophy of education, has had analogous implications in the philosophical field. The 'revolution in philosophy' was in part inspired by a desire to ape the precisions of science; hence its hostility to metaphysics. Hence, too, its concern with language as a contemporary phenomenon. (It is symptomatic of the break in continuity that certain historical aspects in education have acquired a new name; what was traditionally referred to as educational philosophy is today, for purposes of discrimination, referred to as educational theory.)

1

Finally, even history has in some degree changed its role. In former times conceived of as a moral energising force, a source of *exempla* and traditional wisdom, as guide or warning to the present, it has itself become, in the fullness of time, objective and 'scientific', concerned to emphasise the reconstruction of former actuality rather than as serving any *direct* function of enlightenment. Even to Dewey, 'knowledge of the past' was 'the key to understanding the present'; and he advocated what he termed the 'genetic method' in a way which would not recommend itself to many contemporary historians who view the past as something exclusively *sui generis*.

I would reiterate that these developments have been far from unfruitful. Theorising about education (to be distinguished from educational theory) has introduced a degree of intellectual rigour into its study which would have been unthinkable even in the earlier years of my own commitment to teacher training. The psychology of education had made most progress; but what was then termed philosophy was frankly moribund, and sociology of education in its empirical sense practically non-existent. So the reorientations were to be welcomed. Nevertheless, there is some evidence that they, too, are beginning to wear themselves out. Let me first consider philosophy of education. The clarification of educational concepts (primarily) and some attention to ethics and philosophy of mind have had an admirably astringent effect on our thinking about education; but there has been a developing tendency for the subject to become parasitic upon itself. Philosophers have come increasingly to sustain a private conversation among themselves: every effort after analytical precision calls forth rejoinders and counter-rejoinders (think of 'indoctrination'), a process which, given the nature of language and its imprecision, can happily go on for a long time, if not for ever.

No one, I hope, will accuse me of not regarding some of this process as both salutary and invigorating. After all, did I not myself, in my *Freedom and Authority in Education* (1952) call in my amateurish way for a 'probing and prodding of words' so that 'the halt, lame and footsore, those worn out with usage and ripe for retirement, might well be put to hospital and there either nursed back to life or provided with decent burial' (p. 19)? But the time has surely come when the whole debate needs to be seen in part as covertly prescriptive — for the choice of concepts regarded as worthy of extended attention betrays a specific orientation of mind revelatory of certain educational priorities and presumptions as to what is to be regarded as valuable. It is no accident that so much attention should have been paid to concepts such as 'indoctrination', 'autonomy', 'reason' and the like. To view such concepts in their historical context, and to be brought to realise that other educationists in former times not inferior (to say the least) in cultural achievement have emphasised a very different set of concepts is to become apprised of a certain parochialism of philosophical attention which might well benefit from an extended awareness.

The aim of the first and in some respects key essay in this book — 'The parochialism of the present' — is to encourage some such widening of perspective. To see that 'conceptual' philosophy in some degree shares with the other, 'systematic' philosophy an inescapable if less explicit orientation is salutary in itself; to be brought also to realise that other minds, in no way inferior to those at present engaged in the field, fostered a very different set of working concepts might well both help to revivify a flagging analytical attention by bringing to notice relevant but neglected notions such as 'imitation' and at the same time call into question assumptions behind current emphases. The thought that some-one even in the fairly distant past may have had something to say about education worth listening to might well strike some as eccentric in this era of the 'tradition of the new'. But, as more and more philosophers come to see that their subject has reached something of an impasse, I detect the beginnings of an interest in some such view which I attempt to crystallise in that essay.

It is here that I reach back to the beginnings of a phase of European civilisation from which we have quite recently — during this century — emerged. It is certainly arguable that we are beginning to live in an age which can be described as post-Renaissance, so that, for instance, the classical humanism on which for so long we have been sustained is at last beginning to fade from the minds of men; but that is no reason why the memory of it should not be revived for what it can still teach us. The notion that historical phases are so dissimilar as to make the extrapolation of lessons learnt in the one meaningless in another, has always seemed to me an exaggeration. (No doubt such an idea is rein-forced by the current fashion in sociology to regard social and intellec-tual structures as *no more than* the constructs of a particular phase of development.) Clearly insights acquired need careful consideration in the light of changed circumstances. But who, in the practicalities of life does not rely on experience — and what is history but extended experience? The Renaissance period itself and the humanism it fostered provide an illuminating example of the way in which an historical experience — that of the classical world — was assimilated, absorbed and redeployed for creative purposes. And indeed, as I point out in my essay on 'The Arts in Education', the whole history of artistic creativity indicates the vital importance of past models in the creative process, admittedly to be transcended by the greatest minds but not before they have provided a disciplined framework of past experience essential as a propaedeutic to 'originality'. Indeed, the Renaissance theory of art and its emphasis on artifice seems to demonstrate a superior understanding

3

of the processes of creativity to that of the Romantics with its hankering after the new, the original and the untried. This superiority of theoretical understanding may well account for the superiority of even the more mundane products of the Renaissance *botteghe* to the eccentric productions of modern artists fostered by an extreme Romantic individualistic ideology. (When will the art world find its Leavis?)

At the centre of the Renaissance experience, then, there was a literature − that of the classical world. True, 'literature' was slightly differently constituted from what would go under that specific title today − it included history (if often of a semi-mythical variety), political writings and some moral philosophy (provided they were written eloquently and with emotional force) as well as poetry and drama. But it is arguable that today the novel has in some degree replaced those elements which we would no longer include under the heading of literature strictly defined, so that even in its modern guise it constitutes the nearest representative of that central energising force of 'letters' which underwrote the Renaissance experience. (Indeed, the status of the fictional bothered the Renaissance just as much or even more than it does us today − a clear indication that at the core of Renaissance letters was an 'imaginative' experience as today it is at the centre of modern conceptions of literature.)

At any rate, Renaissance understanding of man and society was informed by 'letters', not science. That it achieved a sophistication and depth of insight never in some respects subsequently equalled is indicated by the example of Shakespeare and much else in the painting and poetry of the time. Shakespeare − to take him alone − had genius; but it was brought to fruition by a particular linguistic richness fostered by a humanist training: the man found the language adequate to the profundity of his insight. All this provides support for Leavis's contention in *Education and the University* concerning the centrality of literature in training minds which are subtle and perceptive in the 'important choices of actual life'. Just as philosophy is currently in a state of relative disorientation following the failure to evolve either an unequivocal language or a limitation of the meaningful to what is scientifically verifiable, so the social sciences have become strongly critical of the positivism which has historically informed much of their empirical practice. That there is much educational investigation which can be assisted by the sort of imaginative insight into people's behaviour fostered by good literature is the contention of the essay on 'Literature and the social sciences'. No investigation can produce an outcome superior to the insights implicit in the actual questions asked or the nature of the information sought. It is a noticeable fact that the most fruitful social investigations in the educational field are marked, not by a superiority of purely technical expertise, but by one of imaginative insight. (I would instance the recent investigations into children's linguistic codes[2] and the research on cultural reproduction carried out at the Centre de sociologie européenne[3] to support my contention.) An awareness of the implications of social situations, of men in relationship, can be fostered and enlarged by the insights of great novelists or playwrights.

It is precisely this imaginative insight which has been lacking in much of our positive action in educational organisation in recent years. Historical awareness of the origins of the pressure to equalisation and homogenisation which has marked our reorganisation of secondary schooling reveals it not as the reaction to a little local difficulty over selection, but a manifestation of a deep social and cultural change in our whole way of life. Briefly, the gradual predominance of scientific over traditionally humanistic ways of looking at the world has fostered an increasing homogenisation of social behaviour where, formerly, human differentiation existed in terms of at least a putative qualitative discrimination, for science encourages the consideration of phenomena in terms of isolable, identical 'units' in order to categorise them under general laws. My essay on 'Equality in education' seeks both to explore the historical roots of this urge towards homogenisation and at the same time, in line with a literary appreciation of human potential, suggest a more satisfactory model of human educative possibility based on the notion of equality of concern leading to a necessary differentiation of curricular offering. Today neither the meritocratic nor the egalitarian model offers that liberalisation of mind and activity which must always remain the supreme aim of the educator wedded to the finest tradition of educational prescription the West has produced – a tradition historically analysed and clarified in my essay on 'The idea of a liberal education'. However inadequately the aim of liberalisation is fulfilled, it must always remain an aspiration which transcends the view of man as producer (the meritocratic model) or as social replica (the egalitarian model).

Two other of our current dilemmas are illuminated by historical-literary analysis and consideration. While during the last few years students have become rather more quiescent than they were during the late 1960s and early 1970s, the relative harmony of the generations which reigned during my childhood has disappeared, perhaps for ever. Trade union recalcitrance is merely the most overt manifestation of shifting power relationships within the traditional body politic; and formerly putatively 'disadvantaged' groups – such as students and women – will never again accept their traditional roles unquestioningly. When some years ago I happened to read Turgenev's *Fathers and Sons* I was struck by the prototypical figure of Bazarov in the novel and sensed that an analysis of his situation might have its lessons for the new dispensation. What as yet existed as only a fairly vague adumbration was crystallised by a realisation that Professor Lewis Feuer had noted an analogous appreciation in his work on *The Conflict of Generations*. What Professor Feuer only briefly referred to I now determined to work out more fully – hence my essay 'The death of Bazarov', an analysis which I feel has in no way dated during the present period of relative – and only relative – quiescence; for the basic conflict of the generations, once brought to consciousness with the violence of the late 1960s, must now count as a factor in future staff-student relationships.

Finally, my plea in 'The parochialism of the present' for what I term the 'evocative role of educational theory' receives a practical embodiment in the essay on 'Discovery methods'. There I explore the implications of the method by examining an early recommendation of its usage in Rousseau's *Emile*. Rousseau reveals the fundamental principles more succinctly and at greater depth than subsequent advocates because, like all pioneers, he has to think out his advocacy at a profounder level than those who simply stand on his shoulders; it is these pioneers we should question when we wish to achieve the fullest understanding of what their successors are about. For it is these pioneers who, in educational theory as elsewhere, are the representatives of that historical consciousness which, whether we like it or not, continues to influence our educational practices. If the essays in this book remind us of, and document, that fact, help us to recover a sense of the importance of the historical dimension in deciding what is viable, they will have fulfilled their function.

Chapter 1

The parochialism of the present:
some reflections on the history of educational theory

I do not intend, in this discussion, to get myself involved in the Hirst-O'Connor imbroglio over the different significances which can be attached to the concept 'theory'.[1] I shall simply stipulate that educational theory is to be regarded as essentially prescriptive by nature, concerned to draw on such understanding of a pupil and his circumstances as may seem relevant with a view to pedagogic action; it is, in effect, systematic thought about how to educate people.

In the past, many books have appeared which have taken this as their aim; and the study of some of these works formed part of the initiation of the student teacher into his professional life. Latterly such study has been dropped, partly no doubt because the proliferation of contemporary information arising out of the application of social science techniques to education has produced a seemingly more relevant introduction to the work of the practising teacher. Courses on great educators have, indeed, never been popular; and yet properly handled they can provide an indispensable enrichment to those considerations of value which all teachers, whether they are consciously aware of it or not, must face. That in the past a very different set of teaching priorities prevailed, as is made clear in these important historical documents, challenges the self-evident correctness of current acceptances, at least for the thoughtful. Whereas it is true that social changes enforce some degree of reorientation, there persists at the deeper level a continuity of human problems that makes historical ways of tackling them as 'relevant' as could be wished for. At the very least, they challenge current assumptions and enforce justification rather than mindless acceptance; they constitute an enlargement of pedagogic experience.

In addition, these books have an intrinsic historical interest and help to amplify our specifically historical understanding by revealing the cultural priorities of former times. This is immediately noticeable in

7

the concepts in terms of which they chart their recommendations. Thus, by the seventeenth and eighteenth centuries words like 'reason', 'understanding', 'discovery' and 'method' have a modern ring about them. But prior to that attention was to 'words' rather than 'things' and this fostered a very different set of organising principles.

Words, indeed, were the essential items in the humanists' bill of fare. It is hardly surprising that in a world before movable type had been invented matters relating to communication should have been at the core of the curriculum. The foundations of medieval education had been defined in the *trivium* − grammar, logic and rhetoric. Initiation was through grammar − Latin grammar of course − which dealt with the basic structural aspects of the language; then the scholastics had stressed logic as the means by which the frequently disparate though ancient authoritative pronouncements (in terms of which the Middle Ages defined their understanding of man and God) could either be reconciled or decisively adjudicated between.

It was, however, the study of rhetoric that the humanists stressed in their criticism of the logic-chopping of the scholastics. The boundaries between logic and rhetoric are not always clearly marked; both are concerned with problems of communication and both are intended to assist the maintenance of a specific stance in discourse. In general, however, rhetoric was more popularly oriented, and its highest purpose was to persuade contemporaries to moral truths with a view to the harmonious and fruitful conduct of civic and political life. Whether the political system was oligarchical or princely a training in rhetoric afforded skills considered necessary in the conduct of affairs − as bureaucrat, in the law courts, as courtier, or in local government, in ambassadorial functions, in any social or civic position where words written or spoken had the power to activate, the humanist, in an increasingly politicised society, might find employment. Rhetoric, of course, was initiated in relation to the spoken word and retains its close affiliation with speech during the Renaissance period.[2]

I stress this centrality of the rhetorical training, its growing political importance in the gradual evolution of the increasingly secularised nation or civic state, to emphasise how wrong Durkheim was to see in it little more than a dilettante concern for elegance.[3] Its ideal remained morality in action, whether in the chancelleries of city states or the courts of absolute monarchs, through skill in the persuasive power of language informed by morality. What was the specifically educational implication of the training necessary for so crucial a role?

Clearly it derived from the classical model of the orator explicit in the writings of Cicero and Quintilian; furthermore its central energising discipline was that classical and patristic literature (which included history and political writings) from which were to be derived both moral content and stylistic purity. As a technique intended to train in the art of discourse it was especially influenced by Cicero. The Renaissance study of rhetoric usually involved an analytic approach which examined composition (spoken or written) from the point of view of invention (the process of discovering valid arguments to render a case plausible), arrangement (the structuring of a discourse), style, delivery and memory.

I give this truncated account because I am particularly interested in one feature of it – what is called 'invention', the discovery of appropriate material from the point of view of both style and content. Vergerius had urged that 'thought without style' was not 'likely to attract much notice or secure a sure survival';[4] and indeed, the humanists initiated a revolution in classical studies which was eminently stylistic. But content was equally important: 'Nothing is more admirable', proclaimed Erasmus, 'than discourse abounding in a certain rich *copia* of words or ideas, like a river of gold.'[5] To modern ears, the notion of 'invention' suggests the finding out of something new; to the humanist it implied mainly a searching out of appropriate material from the sources of classical and patristic literature mentioned earlier, literature which formed a repository from which the humanist was usually content to draw both material and form in *imitation* of past models.

The point I wish to establish is that at the centre of the humanists' educational concern was the notion of the 'commonplace', the Latin *locus communis*, the Greek *topos* or topic. Now there are several features of these *topoi* to which I would draw attention. They were, to begin with, essentially moral in character, their most frequent use being in the praise of virtue or the repudiation of vice. In general they comprised storehouses or thesauri of sayings, figures of speech, moral sentences, aphorisms or proverbial saws culled from a variety of sources – but especially, of course, classical authors – which could help sustain or embellish a persuasive argument intended to induce a moral, social, political or legal outcome. Numerous books of such adages arranged under appropriate headings – including Erasmus's own *Adagia* – appeared, and students in schools spent long hours memorising, paraphrasing and amplifying such extracts (as well, of course, as fuller texts) so that they would always provide a ready source of material of use in both the matter and manner of discourse. Thus a typical preface to a commonplace book described it as a 'magazine of choice moral Precepts, grave Admonitions, divine Sentences, with abundance of very edifying and political Maxims for the true regulation of Life and Behaviour'.[6]

This, very briefly and inadequately, is something of the reality which lay behind the humanists' pleas for eloquence and philosophy – by which, of course, they always implied moral philosophy. What I am

9

particularly concerned to bring out is its basic unoriginality, its essentially derivative character, despite the fact that what was intended by 'imitation' was not a *slavish* copying.[7] In this way, the mind was *prepared* for experience; it was not considered that experience should precede instruction. As Erasmus put it, doctors do not learn on their patients how to distinguish between poisons and healing drugs, neither should sailors acquire the art of navigation as a result of shipwrecks. Knowledge of words (*verba*) should take precedence in time over the knowledge of things (*res*). The humanists were responsible for a profound revolution in the education of the ruling classes, for they made literacy and knowledge essential to the arts of government; but knowledge they conceived of primarily as a repository to be acquired rather than as a tool for testing. True, their aim was practical life as they conceived it; but in their view the 'nature' of man was such as to require nurture, and that of a very specific kind. Above all, no time was to be wasted, Erasmus urged, in terms which gave the lie to Rousseau's subsequent injunction; for all humanists saw the need for induction into an historic culture – they were emphatic about history – while Rousseau tried to avoid historical contagion until the last possible moment.

Humanist education, then, as advocated by its theorists and as practised to a considerable degree in its schools, was highly derivative; primarily it involved an induction into a heritage, an assimilation of both the minutiae and content of previous discourse – of word, phrase, sentence, structure and sentiment. It is the opinion of good critics that this intense linguistic training profoundly influenced their practice in, for instance, the arts. Thus the art historian Dr M. Baxandall considers that during the humanist revolution 'experience was being recategorised – through systems of ideas dividing it up into new ways – and so re-organised. . . . They let *verba* influence *res* to an extraordinary degree.'[8] This influence on the actual transitions in painting between the beginning of the fourteenth and that of the sixteenth centuries he traces in his fascinating little books *Painting and Experience* and *Giotto and the Orators*. Hence the emphasis in Renaissance education on imitation and the formation of habits. Hence, too, its sanctification of the notion of artifice. (Puttenham, the literary theorist, regarded 'artificial' as a word of praise: in the Renaissance 'to imitate the excellent artificiality of the most renowned work-masters that antiquity affordeth' constituted the pre-eminent ideal.)[9] Certainly the humanists endorsed the notion of individual differences – 'nihil *Minerva* invita' – nothing contrary to one's natural bent – came aptly to Erasmus's mind as a *topos* worthy of repetition.[10] Furthermore they initiated the belief in man's powers of self-determination apart from the supernatural intervention of grace. But above all, the Renaissance was strongly of the opinion that it is 'natural' to human beings to be artificial, and that the particular form of their self-determination was to be achieved through saturation in an historical culture. This deeply affected their conception of the pedagogic function. It made them unrepentant in their view, derived from a phrase of Cicero's, that the function of education, as of all human impact on the natural world, was to form a 'second nature' different from and superior to the endowments of primitive nature. Hence the unashamed employment of metaphors such as 'moulding' or 'shaping'; hence too their profound appreciation of the need for culture to triumph over the primitive, the given in nature. They had not yet imbibed reductionist notions of 'sincerity' and 'authenticity'; instead they conceived of the world as a stage, and unashamedly sought to present the self in everyday life as a manifestation of artifice. (Stephen Greenblatt in his study of Sir Walter Raleigh provides an excellent picture of how this 'fashioning of the self as a work of art' affected the career and behaviour of his subject.)[11]

This view of the dynamics of the human situation – that the development of consciousness inevitably encompasses a potential for self-consciousness and hence for self-projection, but that that self is best expressed through an internalisation of traditional models as an essential propaedeutic to self-expression – characterises the greatest educational treatise of the Renaissance, *The Book of the Courtier*.

The central core of the *Courtier* is concerned with the process by which the main characteristic of the ideal courtier, 'grace' (*grazia*) is transmuted through art into a *natural* feature of his behaviour – that 'second nature' of which Cicero had spoken. A key passage, spoken by Count Ludovico, runs as follows:[12]

> having already thought a great deal about how this 'grace' is acquired ... I have already discovered a universal rule which seems to apply more than any other in all human actions and words: namely to steer away from affectation at all costs ... and ... to practise in all things a certain nonchalance which conceals all artistry and makes whatever one says or does uncontrived and effortless. ... So we can truthfully say that true art is what does not seem to be an art. ...

The highest art, then, is that which hides art, an art which is manifest in the permeation of the whole behaviour by a grace assumed with an apparent effortlessness (*sprezzatura*). Thus is offered for our consideration a possible consummation of a human, secularised nature which sets out to *achieve* rather than to express what it terms 'naturalness': as I indicated earlier, man's 'nature' is expressed through artifice, the artificial.

I think that this account is worth pondering for several reasons. It reveals, to begin with, an ambiguity at the heart of the concept of

11

'naturalness', a concept which plays a crucial role in so many theories of education. 'Naturalness' is today often equated with the artless rather than, as in Castiglione, the artful. (I use 'artful' to imply simply the product of artifice without any of those pejorative overtones the word has today — perhaps symptomatically — with implications such as 'they must be taking us in', 'too clever by half'.) Behind these differences lie two opposed conceptions of 'nature', one teleologically conceived, the other deliberately denuded of certain qualitative attributes so as to make quantitative scrutiny more possible; these latter procedures are inevitably reductionist, for the phenomena must be stripped of certain distinguishing differences, so as to enable a formulaic abstraction to be made. The former view is inevitably normative, the other intentionally neutral.

Furthermore, 'effortlessness' is intended to imply mastery through effort, 'spontaneity' arising out of a highly wrought discipline, not that of primitive impulse. Nothing in Castiglione would encourage the notion that 'the first impulses of nature are always right.'[13] Hence we find in Castiglione's methodology a surprising paradox — these attributes of the courtier, so expressive of something liberated, free flowing, stem not from the triumph of impulse but the constrictions of 'imitation':[14]

> Therefore anyone who wants to be a good pupil must not only do things well but must also make a constant effort to imitate and, if possible, exactly reproduce his master. And when he feels he has made some progress it is very profitable for him to observe different kinds of courtiers and . . . take various qualities now from one man and now from another.

It is not that judgment has no role to play — the courtier's assimilation must be 'ruled by the good judgment that must always be his guide' — but to achieve the highest human attribute of 'grace' it has to be exercised within a limited area of choice and depends on assimilation to a previous model. This is not the autonomous judgment but one which makes discriminations within the area of the 'given'.

It is interesting that contemporary theories of painting employed very much the same set of concepts to distinguish excellence as Castiglione used to distinguish the finest attributes of man. Thus Vasari found in Michelangelo's statutes 'the most graceful of all grace' and in Leonardo a *grazia divina*.[15] Similar notions of ease and facility and similar ideas of drawing on attributes from several sources in order to correct the imperfections of individual appearances mark both the art of making images and pictures and that of making men, so that the result in both cases at once exploits a common experience and yet produces something which transcends the everyday. Put another way, these ways of fashioning both absorb the given and yet seek to transcend it. It is not simply that man is to become a work of art − it is that in the process he is to surpass the primitive and the mundane. In this way he could actualise his 'nature', either as painter or as man. Yet in both cases he depended on processes of *imitation*. In both cases he merited the definition of his activities in the words of the mid-sixteenth-century theorist of art as 'an artificial imitation of Nature'.[16]

Finally it is necessary to draw attention to the range of activities through which the courtier was to express his role. They comprised manners and morals as well as knowledge, physical and warlike exercises as well as learning. It was a total education, in fact, springing out of the amalgamation of the medieval chivalric tradition with that of the Renaissance humanist. Manners, military prowess, graceful movement, intellectual or artistic pursuits and moral understanding all infused with that grace which constituted their expressive excellence and directed to the influencing of the prince in the ways of virtue and hence contributing to the health of the whole society − essentially, that is, for instrumental purposes − these contributed to the delineation of an ideal man of action.

But as the exposition unfolds itself to modern ears, is there not an uneasy feeling that they must have got it all hideously wrong? They were, of course, elitist, although, with a certain reluctance, they were willing to recruit high talent when of lowly birth, as Sir Thomas Elyot makes clear. They advocated imitation of the best models − not a word, methodologically, about creativity or autonomy. Their recommendation of a literary training was founded and sustained on the opinions, advocacies, figurative usages and sententious sayings of others − the commonplace rather than the original. Their methodological stress was primarily on memory (they sometimes sought to train an artificial memory). Their world was consciously a stage and their products players; and as players, it seems, the emphasis was on learning rather than on improvising their parts. Certainly, any improvisation could only arise out of a profound absorption of previous achievements.

Of course, like all curricular models, it was flawed: men 'began to hunt more after words than matter';[17] and, where matter was concerned, it was manifest as 'feigned history' by which it 'submitted the shows of things to the desires of the mind.'[18] But what if the desires were evil? This vast apparatus of rhetoric could so easily serve the ends of wicked men. Too easily the 'drossy age' doted on those who 'only got the ... *outward* habit of encounter.' Little wonder that there was plenty of anti-courtier literature, condemning the 'base sycophants, crumb-catching parasites'.[19] Shakespeare's major theme relates to human appearance and human reality − note Iago's 'I am not what I am,' Lady Macbeth's 'Look like the innocent flower, but be the serpent under't,' the pervasive presence of disguise in his plays. Time and again, he reveals the deceits of speech — 'Words are grown false' and have become the tools of deceitful men.

So this education failed to achieve the virtue it aimed at and, simultaneously, the terms of its advocacy fly in the face of all our aspirations after autonomy, creativity, freedom of expression and reasoning after the modern, impersonal model. Instead it stressed imitation, authority, judgment for persuasive purposes, memory and the acceptance of traditional models. Not surprisingly, Bacon urged that 'it is not good to stay too long in the theatre.' (There were, of course, other social reasons for its decline — but this implied quarrel with what came to be regarded as 'truth' played an important part.)

Yet the mention of Shakespeare introduces an ambiguous note into this condemnation. For the paradox is that the greatest dramatist the world has ever known, the man who more than any other has explored the sheer range of human kind was the product of this humanist education. Shakespeare could not have written as he did without his rhetorical training; we know, because modern scholarship has discovered the sources — many of them the commonplaces — of his greatest verbal triumphs. We have the paradox that this apparently oppressive educational regimen helped to produce the facility and effortlessness of creativity — a paradox which, as Professor Baldwin points out, 'Shakespeare shares with his age'; he 'never originated anything ... and yet he is one of the most original authors who has ever lived.'[20]

Not only did Shakespeare derive his incredible verbal facility, his acute awareness of the nuances of speech, from his humanist training for projection into his vast range of characters; he also benefited enormously from another feature of Renaissance education — its inheritance of the basically medieval procedure of disputation, argumentation and debate, which fostered the ability to see differing viewpoints. Indeed, he 'fully shared the Elizabethan delight in building up both sides of an argument'[21] — a procedure which the rhetorical and logical training of the schools fostered.

The rest of Renaissance culture in art and sculpture, architecture, even music, made it one of the greatest creative periods in the history of man. How come that this fecundity was accompanied by a system of education so repressive, derivative, authoritarian, even brutal (although, here, the humanists, within a well-disciplined framework, sought to mitigate the physical harshness of the schools)? Is it that systems of education just do not matter? Hardly: we have the minutely documented case of Shakespeare to indicate the contrary.

One might question further. The replacement of humanism by the early development of the autonomous, cognitive style during the

14

seventeenth and eighteenth centuries (earlier adumbrations of this can be identified in the educational theorising of Vives and Montaigne where men are encouraged directly to confront 'experience' untransmuted by literary treatment) would seem to have been accompanied by a process of verbal and linguistic attrition (except, of course, in the invention of technical terms). It is a style which has evolved, with its characteristic stress on what it has been pleased to identify as experience rather than on traditional authority, on things rather than on words, on certain types of reasoning of which 'a paradigm case', we have been recently assured,[22] is the scientific and which has implied the 'transcendence of the particular' as opposed to the particularised audience orientation of Renaissance persuasiveness. An early symptom of certain types of verbal deprivation can be detected in Bishop Sprat's *History of the Royal Society*, with its plea against 'the luxury and redundancy of speech' and its injunction to 'bring all things as near the mathematical plainness, as they can: and prefer the language of Artisans, Countrymen, and Merchants, before that of Wits, or Scholars.' This process of attrition was, of course, prolonged and intricate and cannot be adequately chronicled here. It implied the death of the verse drama, the emergence of the novel with, initially at least, an expansion in individuation and psychological realism but compounded of narrative written in a prose 'which restricts itself, almost entirely, to a descriptive and denotative use of language.'[23] The characters no longer speak with the individual flexibility which marked Elizabethan verse, but more with the voice of the writer – as an acute critic noted of the characters of Henry James.[24] A further related development has been the reductionism characteristic of so much modern writing, with the restriction of range implied – what Henry James referred to, in his comment on the French naturalists: *'ces messieurs* seem to have lost the perception of anything in nature but the genital organs,'[25] and which Professor Duncan Williams has documented in his book *The Trousered Ape*.

Such a process of attrition would seem to have culminated in our own times in the most serious consequences for the range and quality of our artistic life and, hence, for aspects of truth about the world. The new cognitive style, implicit in the stress by educationists on things rather than on words, is one directed to the elucidation of physical behaviour for predictive purposes and to the domination of the physical environment. Whether, in fact, the characteristic features of this type of reasoning do really mirror, at all points, the procedures of scientists is open to doubt, as I shall indicate. But it is a style of reasoning, on a putative scientific model, that has gone far to replace, in the conduct of human affairs, the type of judgment the humanists deployed in their search for arguments (their invention, in the sense defined), and their use of language in a human context of persuasion and advocacy. For their rhetorical purposes, the humanists advocated an immersion in a wide heterogeneity of writings — and the techniques of writing — which, to those capable of assimilation, enforced a multiplicity of viewpoints, a kaleidoscope of impressions and an attention to language in its full cognitive-emotive range (in contrast to the denotative use advocated by many later theorists). In these ways they conveyed something of the texture of human life in all its multiplicity. It was quite extraordinarily eclectic.

Contrast some of the implications of the new style of reasoning which was to replace humanistic *judicatio* (judgment) on language and content. It became the tool of the Baconian impulse to obey nature as a prelude to its domination, from which, indeed, it gathered its initial characteristic of impartiality and objectivity. (We note this in Bacon's criticism of the Idols.) Transposed to the human world after the manner advocated increasingly since the seventeenth century there is an implied assimilation of the human to the world of 'things' — of objects — for prediction and manipulation. It is not altogether surprising that the originator of the world's most extensive totalitarian system should have thought of himself as applying scientific method to society. It is arguable that the outcome belongs to the pathology of science; but it is important to realise the dangers of historico-scientific prediction in its temptation to energise its finding through the imposition of intellectual abstractions on the living complexity of actual peoples in pursuit of the stated attempt to change the world.

In identifying more fully the general orientation of mind involved (too close detail would encounter ambiguities in the accounts given) we may note such characteristics as the pursuit of the 'end-in-view', problem isolation by means of analysis, demands for evidence or 'good reasons' and the expectation of solutions. Thus a general delineation of current intellectual work runs as follows:[26]

> If he can do intellectual work at all, he knows what it is to get
> something wrong, and he knows what it is to be in a muddle; and,
> knowing this, he also cares, however slightly, about getting things
> right and getting things sorted out.

In general this use of reason works by a process of abstraction, as in the scientific field it necessitated the early discrimination of primary and secondary qualities. Hence, in its application to the human field, the emphasis has necessarily fallen on the uniform and the typical — 'typification' is part of the process advocated by the sociologist Alfred Schutz in his creation of the 'ideal type'. And part of the effect of statistical manipulations is to lose sight of the eccentric, the idiosyncratic and the individual. There is no difficulty, in the conduct of human affairs, in finding problems — for, given the imperfections of

16

the human situation, they can be identified at the drop of a hat. What one has to judge — and this implies processes of imaginative projection where the 'evidence' is often of an extremely flimsy kind, analogous to something as vague as one's 'feeling for life' in all its multivariate complexity — is what problems one ought to learn to live with and which are likely to yield to amelioration. Talk of solutions, of 'getting things right', except where comparative trivialities are concerned, is usually evidence of the assimilation of human to scientific or mathematical problems to which they often bear little resemblance. (I would instance the controversy over the 11+ as a good example of the way in which unrealistic assessments of stresses and outcomes has induced unfortunate policies.)

The whole process is intended to foster a critical spirit and an autonomous cognitive style. I will say something of the latter later; the former is much vaunted educationally. Thus we are informed — God help us! — that[27]

> to exhibit a critical spirit one must be alert to the possibility that the established norms themselves ought to be rejected, that the rules ought to be changed, the criteria used in judging performances modified. Or even that the mode of performance ought not to take place at all.

This, apparently, is what teaching a *child* to be critical may imply. It seems to be recognised that children cannot become morally autonomous until there has been some initiation into the rules. It does not seem to be appreciated to the same extent that a prolonged process of cultural initiation is necessary before criticism can in any way become meaningful. How can one significantly criticise the rules until one has achieved a high level of saturation in their implications and meaning? The very concept of a rule in many cultural areas raises inappropriate expectations of a formulaic rendition foreign to the subtlety and complexity of the disciplines involved. How can one criticise 'norms' unless one has some sense of their significance and working? This applies even if the process of criticism is dignified with the appellation 'critico-creative thinking' as a protection against any imputation that what is intended is merely destructive criticism. It should, however, be recalled that, historically, the spirit of criticism *has* been deeply concerned with 'clearing the ground a little, and removing some of the rubbish'.[28] Scepticism seems to be directed against what already exists whereas scepticism about the benefits of projected change might prove more beneficial. The difficulty with the 'under labourer's' view has become that it all too readily encourages manifestations of cultural bulldozing. (There is, of course, a place in relevant circumstances for pedagogic stimulation by appropriate questionings within the disciplines.

17

But this is something very different from the questioning of the norms.)

I suggest that one of the outcomes of studying the history of educational theory is that it stimulates the asking of such and analogous questions. For the recommendations made at least imply outcomes as they themselves spring out of changed orientations, social and cultural. If humanism initiates or at least accompanies a particular phase of aristocratic culture – a time when writing, as Castiglione puts it, was still a kind of speech – the back-up in the schools, where the broad recommendations are translated into some sort of actuality, can be seen to offer certain kinds of cultural opportunity. Humanism, with its human rather than divine orientations, provided the linguistic subtlety that permitted ever profounder explorations of the world of man – social, political, individual, imagistic. To probe such educational recommendations is to enter on a range of possibilities and actualities revelatory, in this case, of a very different articulation from that of our own. To feed this in to current preoccupations is not to expect a reversal, but at least a possible enrichment, of contemporary modes. It should at least be allowed to count as 'evidence', so that we are encouraged, for instance, to pay more attention to cultural saturation and less to advocacies of autonomy and the spirit of criticism.[29]

It can be allowed to count for more. Mention of the world of 'things' can be allowed to gentle us into the clarificatory rather than the evocative role of educational theory, one that works by assimilation rather than contrast. What I have identified so far is the gradual assimilation of the human to the world of things. In the light of Rousseau's *Emile* the analysis achieves a degree of corroborative evidence. Rousseau as much as any one put paid educationally to the old world and ushered in a new phase. (Locke was still partly in the courtier tradition and tempers 'enlightenment' with a concern for traditional manners and morals.) But Rousseau's intent is to lay a firm basis before socialisation, largely on the grounds that in this way the young will be protected from current corruptions; he thus resolutely places the young Emile in the world of things and insists even that his first human non-moral contacts shall arise out of those most closely related to this world. Indeed he gets near to treating Emile himself as a thing, denuding him in his social isolation of opportunities for acquiring a rudimentary sense of morality, protecting him from the emotional life, avoiding habit and, in true Enlightenment style, 'prejudice'. His analysis of the fable of the fox and the crow is very revealing in its demand for a certain category of literalness and its total insensitivity to a sort of discourse highly nutritive to children. His educational recommendation amounts to an injunction to serve and understand the child while subjecting him to ceaseless manipulation – much like Bacon's obedience for mastery. He seeks to turn Emile into a young technologist, teaching him the need to observe the iron law of necessity by keeping him dependent on things while initiating him into the regularities of their behaviour. Symptomatically he lifts his ban on books — 'reading, the curse of childhood' — to permit a perusal of *Robinson Crusoe* which could be regarded as every man's survival kit in primitive surroundings. It is the technological urge that in effect Rousseau seeks to stimulate, manipulating the environment in pursuit of that balance of power and desire which he regards as his ultimate educational aim.

There are, of course, two Emiles, although in terms of subsequent effect this first one — with its emphasis on sense-experience, discovery, environmental stimuli and exploration, teacher abnegation, child observation, all feeding into progressive theorising — has not only a succinctness and a mastery of expression that marks it off from the long-windedness and uncertainties of the adolescent phase, but is also deeply revealing of certain aspects of modernity. (Once Rousseau gets Emile into society he really does not know what to do with him.) What characterised the humanists — verbal richness, personal persuasiveness, moral content, instruction preceding experience, reliance on past authority and induction into a heritage — are to be overturned completely in favour of strict verbal limitation in line with experience which should *precede* instruction, impersonal law, necessity rather than morality as a guide to conduct, the elimination of all previous witness and the consequent fresh start.

Here surely we have a prototype of that individualistic epistemology, that image of the 'cognitively self-made' that Antony Quinton defined in his 'Authority and autonomy in knowledge'. Its connection with the pioneer capitalist-technologist is hinted at in another paragraph of that article; and Mr Quinton's identification of a 'Crusonian story of initially solitary knowers' makes the cross-referencing with Rousseau's young learner peculiarly felicitous. It also reveals the falsity of Rousseau's model, for Mr Quinton rightly considers that in the order of development 'Belief is historically, as well as logically, prior to knowledge'; Rousseau's sacrifice of so much of the humanity of a child — summed up as 'morality', habit and feeling as well as social contact — glaringly fails even in its limited endeavour, for it is against 'belief' as a social phenomenon that he is concerned to protect Emile.[30]

Why then bother with something so inept? The reason is because the writings of theorists like Rousseau are peculiarly revealing. All educational learning models are likely to prove inadequate to the complexity of human development, whether humanistic or scientific in orientation; words deceive, things limit drastically. But writers like Rousseau reveal fundamental principles in terms of which a model is constructed and hence clarify, even in exaggeration, aspects of its structure. Modern expositions of autonomous 'active' learning from the environment parrot the methodological devices without revealing the assumptions on which the model rests. To have these revealed is not only clarifica- tory – it also assists assessment of their viability.

We may say, then, that the historical study of educational theory, if handled correctly, can contribute to intellectual culture as a corrective to the parochialism of the present and at the same time elucidate current admonitions and practices. Modern educational philosophy would appear to be deeply imbued with a commitment to the centrality of mind and knowledge through the acquisition of concepts and their deployment in critical assessment of the environment, human and physical, as a mark of individual autonomy. Approved words, in addi- tion to those just enunciated, include concepts like 'freedom', 'rational', 'liberal', 'public', 'experience'. Current complacency is, or should be, disturbed by encountering a different mental geography whose topo- graphical features may include such notions as 'moulding', 'imitation', 'habit', 'memory', 'invention' (in the sense of recall rather than crea- tion), 'customary', 'authoritative', 'art' (as artifice) and 'grace', and being forced to recognise that such apparent stultifications at least in some degree contributed to a cultural richness which, in its specific fields, our modern age cannot even begin to emulate. This is in no way to deprecate what philosophy of education has achieved within its own universe of discourse; it is simply to suggest that there are other universes which conceivably merit attention.

To be specific, we might be led to question this current stress on 'autonomy' as a desirable educational aim and see it merely as the out- come of a specific tradition of disengagement from traditional norms in the spirit of the Enlightenment. In the perspective of the profound cultural achievements of the Renaissance and of the conditions which nurtured these triumphs of the human spirit the peculiar *emphasis* on autonomy can be seen as a prescription for cultural catastrophe. Great cultures indeed thrive on a basis of imitation and an initial assimilation to habits of use and wont – of saturation, as I have called it. What is possible in the way of autonomy for those capable of 'originality' are relatively small adaptations arising out of and through a thorough assimilation of traditional norms.

We see this in the humanistic culture of the Renaissance as in fact I believe we see it in the scientific culture of our own day. It is part of the false mythology of science – fostered incidentally by educationists like John Dewey – to see it as in a constant process of reconstruction. The readaptations of science are rare excursions – as in the artistic culture of the Renaissance – from the mass of routine work, the continuity of problems permitting a 'low rate of occurrence of really great modifications'. My quotation is from Professor Gerald Holton's

Thematic Origins of Scientific Thought where he compares science to a 'growing organism analogous to a biological species', stressing the elements of continuity and multiplicity of effort as more customary than that of mutation.[31] Holton considers that 'the intellectual discipline imposed upon the physical scientist is now quite as rigorously defined as the conventionalised form for research papers.' The proportion of originality among the current intense activity of scientists is likely to be roughly analogous to that arising out of the humanist training of the Renaissance period. In both cases occasional mutations – to adapt Holton's metaphor – arise out of heavily routinised and conventionalised scientific and literary operations, dependent on forms of 'imitation' rather than anything identifiable as original endeavour. But in both cases this heavily routinised and conventionalised activity, arising out of a saturation in the modes of the two procedures, not only maintains a sound level of ordinary productivity, but forms the essential jumping off place for high achievement. It constitutes a tradition of working which affords opportunities for the genuinely creative mind.

The catastrophic decline in artistic standards in our own day – manifest in any great public gallery of our times – is the result of an excessive stress on autonomy and the decline in the assimilation of any tradition, the almost total elimination of the craftsman's outlook. Let the greatest of twentieth-century artists spell it out: 'But as soon as art had lost all link with tradition, and the kind of liberation that came in with Impressionism permitted every painter to do what he wanted to do, painting was finished.'[32] Until we recapture the need for *training* as a necessary precursor to education we shall be lost. This is the lesson of the Renaissance and, despite popular opinion to the contrary, of the success of science in our own day. In addition to his other deficiencies, the young, humanly autonomous Emile constitutes a quite false model of the necessary conditions for discovery.

Those who have accompanied me so far will detect that I am uttering a plea both for more attention to history and, as outcome of that attention, a suggestion of some dissatisfaction with the range within which current philosophical scrutiny tends to operate. In his essay on Bentham, J.S. Mill urges that[33]

> Nobody's synthesis can be more complete than his analysis. If in his survey of human nature and life he has left any element out, then, wheresoever that element exerts any influence his conclusions will fail, more or less, in their application.

And he adds, to the detriment of Bentham's 'contempt . . . of all other schools of thinkers' of which he speaks a little later, and which he diagnoses as a 'deficiency of imagination',[34]

21

it must be allowed, that even the originality which can, and the
courage which dares, think for itself, is not a more necessary part of
the philosophical character than a thoughtful regard for previous
thinkers and for the collective mind of the human race.

The current excessive emphasis on rationality needs to be tempered by
the realisation that emotion, movement, manners, even gesture have
played their part in other models of the educated man, that words have
not always been tied to impersonal reason or denotation, that the
acceptance of a heritage has a role to play as well as the critical scrutiny
of it, that the stress on innovation and originality is ill-served by a
repudiation of what alone can stimulate their production, an appren-
ticeship spent among the known and the accepted.[35]

The hardiest assertor . . . of the freedom of private judgment . . . is
the very person who needs to fortify the weak side of his own
intellect, by study of the opinions of mankind in all ages and
nations, and of the speculations of philosophers of the modes of
thought most opposite to his own. . . . A man of clear ideas errs
grievously if he imagines that whatever is seen confusedly does not
exist; it belongs to him, when he meets with such a thing, to dispel
the mist, and fix the outlines of the vague form which is looming
through it.

Modern philosophers of education are fond of appealing to a mysterious entity known as the 'public' — 'public criteria', 'public symbols',
'public meaning': 'The irreconcilability of the use of reason with
egocentricity and arbitrariness is a reflection of its essentially public
character'[36] we read. But how is this 'public' constituted? Does it
include 'past thinkers' and 'the collective mind of the human race'? It is
to be hoped so, for an appeal to this wide source of enlightenment
might have the effect of enlarging our notions of reason to permit the
incorporation of something I would perhaps prefer to call judgment —
a sort of up-dated version of the *judicatio* of the humanists, to assimilate later versions of literary procedure. Characteristic of 'judgment' in
this revised sense would be the recognition that human problems
cannot always be defined with the clarity and distinctness fostered by a
putative scientific approach, that often they need to be seen as part of
a network of meanings to which their relationship is organic, not
mechanical, and where disturbance in one part of the system may well
have repercussions unanticipated by a procedure adapted more to
things than to human beings. 'Judgment' will also involve an imaginative projection into the human implications of any proposed 'solution'
— which it will recognise not as a 'solution' but as, at best, an attempted
amelioration. Nurtured by the realisation, as is the great novelist, of the

complexity of human beings, it will the more willingly accept the need for what Keats called 'negative capability', the capacity to be in 'uncertainties, mysteries, doubts without any irritable reaching after fact and reason'. It will thus avoid the incipient perfectionism which clings to notions of rational outcome and will be the less confident in its critical identification of the 'rubbish' it seeks to clear away. For its relationship to the historical past will not be that implicit in any notion of 'cognitive autonomy', but rather one betokening a willingness to incorporate a past and sometimes unfashionable wisdom into any modifications necessitated by the flux of human events. Furthermore, it will admit the efficacy of what might be termed 'know-how' — something only half consciously acquired within specific areas as part of a process of assimilation rather than as a result of conscious decision-making. The appropriate image will not be that of the lonely voyager, the Crusonian isolate living his autonomous cognitive life, but that of the most recent inhabitant of a great estate from the walls of whose mansion emanate reminders of former states of civility not wholly to be dismissed in the search for such evanescent satisfactions as this life affords.[37]

Chapter 2

Literature and the social sciences:
with particular reference to the sociology of education

Literature is of many different kinds, from the intimately personal lyric to the epic which celebrates a national or even (as in *Paradise Lost*) a cosmic theme. It has many different purposes – from the desire to give delight to the intention of informing the moral consciousness. In this paper the literature which is relevant is that concerned with the inter-relationships between people, one which thus overtly, or by implication at least, creates a social world. There is certainly plenty of it – prac-tically all novels and plays and a fair amount of dramatic or narrative poetry. Indeed, only the purely introspective lyric would be quite irrelevant. Furthermore, the sort of literature of this social type is that which focuses, through its offering of characters and incidents – 'an imitation of an action', to use the Aristotelian phrase – the highest consciousness of the age in which it was written. We have here studies of the 'complexities, potentialities and essential conditions of human nature' as such nature orients itself to its fellows, conflicts or co-operates with them, loves or hates in a social world. My brief quota-tion is from Dr Leavis – and another way of indicating the selection of literature I am referring to would be to point to the tradition of writers he has identified in his criticism. To particularise among novelists, let us say the 'great tradition' of Jane Austen, George Eliot, Henry James, Joseph Conrad, D.H. Lawrence – among others, but chiefly these. For Leavis has always seen in literature an extreme expression of the human – and humane – consciousness; and it is this high consciousness that I need.

Now, there are clearly two ways in which the sort of literature I have defined may be said to have some sort of interest for the social scientist.[1] In the first place such works are the products of minds working in a certain social environment, subject to certain influences and pressures;

they are therefore likely to bear witness to these influences and to provide evidence about their nature. To take an obvious example, the writings of C.P. Snow might be thought to provide interesting evidence about the nature and workings of certain sorts of social groupings – academic and scientific, for instance. I would not want to deny that his novels, treated with caution because of their fictional element, might indeed by used by sociologists in this way, and that they might reveal interesting data about the behaviour of committees (say) which would have much the same sort of interest for contemporary social scientists that Dickens has for historians. Clearly there would be pitfalls in using a writer of fiction in this particular sort of way; but I think they are fairly obvious ones, and as this is, in any case, not the only sort of interest a writer can have and is not the one in which I am most interested, I will not go into them.

For indeed, I think that the main interest which creative writers might well have for those concerned with social analysis lies not so much in the incidentals they use as part of the machinery of their fictions but in the very process and consequent effects of their creation of characters interacting in an independent social world. I will argue that this process bears some relationship, which it will be interesting to consider in some detail, to the ways in which some social scientists have conceived their task (notably those who have sought an 'imaginative' or, 'interpretive', understanding – *verstehen* – and especially the late Alfred Schutz), and that practice in penetration into these worlds through the disciplined application of the literary critical intelligence could perhaps have a salutary effect on social investigation, especially in the sphere of education. I believe, too, that such practice might draw attention to some of the present shortcomings of such investigations.

Let me begin by indicating some features of the creative process, as imaginative writers have themselves witnessed to it. Now, it is perfectly true that many imaginative writers would agree with Hardy's statement of the 'real, if unavowed, purpose of fiction' as the desire 'to give pleasure by gratifying the love of the *uncommon* in human experience' (my italics). Nevertheless, it is highly significant that Hardy should proceed by urging that this purpose is most likely to be achieved when the novelist persuades the reader of the 'truth' of his people. Now, in the tradition of writing to which I have drawn attention earlier, 'truth' of a sort is very much the creative writer's aim and indeed constitutes his major claim to our interest. It is important to begin with this point lest the overtly fictional nature of the writer's task might induce a sense of irrelevance in the minds of those whose first task is, after all, the attempt to understand the reality of things. It is true that the very nature of the artistic effort involves the inevitability of some distortion; but, then, paradoxically, so does that of the social scientist, as I shall hope to show.

Let me begin, however, by making clear the nature of literary intent. I shall do this, in two stages. I shall first indicate how a writer in the 'great tradition' saw his task and reported on it during the process of fulfilling it. I shall then analyse a piece of literature to indicate the nature of the finished product.

Any art — that of the novelist included — involves a selective process. As Henry James remarked in his notebooks, life was capable of 'nothing but splendid waste' — 'Life being all inclusion and confusion, and art being all discrimination and selection.' Now, James gives us many more insights into the nature of the novelist's task — no other great writer has been so endlessly curious about the theory of his craft or has reported at such length on its practice. And we become rapidly aware that despite its wastefulness 'life' was by no means irrelevant to his concerns. At the simplest level, for instance, he speaks of his novel *The Princess Casamassima* as having 'proceeded quite directly . . . from the habit and the interest of walking the streets' of London: the hero of that novel 'sprang up for me out of the London pavement.' And in his notebooks there are constant hints which indicate quite clearly that, wasteful though life might be, it was the constant ultimate source of reference. I don't mean simply that he carried home from dinner parties hints and anecdotes which could be worked up into stories and novels; I mean that his constant appeal, in the very process of the working, is to psychological and social reality — and that often at the simplest level. A couple of examples will illustrate what I mean: 'I must make my young man, an Englishman, a clerk in the foreign office . . . one of those competent, colourless, gentlemanly mediocrities of whom one sees so many in London.'[2] And again:[3]

> One sketches one's age but imperfectly if one doesn't touch on that particular matter: the invasion, the impudence and shamelessness, of the newspaper and the interviewer, the devouring *publicity* of life, the extinction of all sense between public and private.

The point is, I hope, taken. But, of course, it is necessary to see the novelist at work more intimately than is provided by such brief snippets. I will therefore take the second extract and show how James's concern for a particular feature of his world came to take on dramatic significance in his mind. My quotation will necessarily be a long one; and, although in the final version of the incident which forms the core of his story a good deal was altered, the extract provides an entirely characteristic example of James's procedure.

London, Thursday, November 17th, 1887.

Last winter, in Florence, I was struck with the queer incident of

26

Miss McC.'s writing to the New York *World* that inconceivable letter about the Venetian society whose hospitality she had just been enjoying – and the strange *typicality* of the whole thing. She acted in perfect good faith and was amazed and felt injured and persecuted, when an outcry and an indignation were the result. That she *should* have acted in good faith seemed to me to throw much light upon that mania for publicity which is one of the most striking signs of our times. She was perfectly irreflective and irresponsible, and it seemed to her pleasant and natural and 'chatty' to describe, in a horribly vulgar newspaper, the people she had been living with and their personal domestic arrangements and secrets. . . . One sketches one's age but imperfectly if one doesn't touch on that particular matter: the invasion, the impudence and shamelessness, of the newspaper and the interviewer, the devouring *publicity* of life, the extinction of all sense between public and private. It is the highest expression of the note of 'familiarity', the sinking of *manners*, in so many ways, which the democratization of the world brings with it. . . . [It] struck me [as] a very illustrative piece of contemporary life – the opposition of the scribbling, publishing, indiscreet, newspaperized American girl and the rigid, old-fashioned, conservative, still shockable and much shocked little society she recklessly plays the tricks upon. The drama is in the consequences for *her*. . . . They are greatest if the thing brings about a crisis and a cataclysm in her 'prospects' . . . the question of her marriage. Imagine the girl engaged to a young Italian or Frenchman of seductive 'position' . . . and then imagine her writing to a blatant American newspaper 'all about' the family and domestic circle of her fiancé, and you have your story.

James then continues to indicate how he will handle his theme. What he has related so far provides the germ of the subject; treatment requires a somewhat different cast, so that he can convey the essence of the original and at the same time avoid any imputation of simply copying. So he invents a young, innocent American girl, engaged to a young European who 'has been brought up and lived wholly *dans les vieilles idées*' and to whom she becomes engaged. A former suitor, a journalist with whom nevertheless she remains on good terms, gets her to reveal the secrets of the family into which she is marrying so that he can use it for his journal:

He of course hasn't a grain of delicacy in his composition (I must do him very well); he has no tradition of reserve or discretion – he simply obeys his gross newspaper instinct. . . . She is simple, sweet, uncultivated, gentle, innocent. . . . He means no harm in pumping her, and she means no harm in telling all about her prospective circle.

27

The resulting revelations, published in 'his big catchpenny newspaper' are read by the young fiancé who thus sees his personal facts and family secrets 'blazoned forth in the vulgarest terms'. The girl, confronted by the consequences of her indiscretion, is too innocent really to grasp the nature of her 'crime'; but irked by the rumpus she has created, she throws up her engagement. 'The end is a little difficult to determine. I think the truest and best and most illustrative would be this': the journalist, learning of the scandal he has brought about, forces a reconciliation on the parties by threatening further revelations of the way the family have treated the girl. So the parents are forced to come round: 'The newspaper dictates and triumphs — which is a reflection of actual fact.'[4]

I would draw attention to James's stress on the 'strange *typicality* of the whole thing.' The theme should possess a representative quality. The emphasis on purely private and personal experience in literature is of very recent origin — it indicates, indeed, a decadence of Romanticism and is representative of a crisis in civilisation rather than characteristic of the normal relationship between writer and public. The early Romantics worked a new vein, but one intended to awaken a corresponding chord of feeling in the reader: as Wordsworth put it 'To this knowledge which all men carry about with them ... the Poet principally directs his attention.' And the notion of generality was at the centre of classical literary theorising: 'Nothing can please many, and please long,' thought Dr Johnson, 'but just representations of general nature.'

I have dwelt a little on this point because it will be of considerable importance for my theme. Not all literature is of the same type, as I have indicated. But in literature of the sort I have in mind concern for the central human problems of the age is crucial. For the moment I wish to pursue further James's handling of the issue which a newspaper incident has aroused in his mind.

Miss McC.'s article throws light, for him, on a characteristic feature of current social life — the impact of 'newspaperization' and its consequent effect on manners and social assumptions. Of particular interest is the discrepancy between what James clearly thinks of the central incident — the betrayal of confidences, the sheer vulgarity of the whole incident — and the triumph of 'impersonality' which his projection of the story represents. By 'impersonality' in this context I refer to his capacity to realise the essential 'innocence' of the offender — the young girl — as well as the shock and indignation of the offended. His literary integrity (and imagination) makes him see that the conflict is not simply one of black and white but a much more complex one involving a difference of national and social milieux, as well as of comparative sophistication on the part of the protagonists. There is not one, but two focal points to the projected story — a sympathetic projection into the diverse consciousness of both parties, and of the moral dilemmas in which they find themselves; and at the same time there is not simply supine acquiescence in the fact of moral difference but a revelation of moral standpoint in the condemnation of the newspaperman. Even here, with the injunction 'I must do him very well,' it is clear that, for all his vulgarity, 'He means no harm in pumping her.' The morality of great art is never simple and unequivocal. Indeed, this capacity for sympathy — expounded in terms of different assumptions of consciousness and an awareness of different gradations of social influence — for standpoints which are yet clearly repugnant to the writer constitutes one of the major educative influences which literature can bring to bear. For literature is neither politics nor preaching (with their offerings of *partis pris*) but an exploratory instrument which offers, among other riches, revelation of the complexities of consciousness.

Now, of course, in the extract from James's notebooks which I have quoted we are given simply a summary of the dramatic conflict as its possibilities begin to reveal themselves to the artistic sensibility. We are told about the incident; it is not presented to us. The abstractions — 'the opposition of the scribbling, publishing, indiscreet, newspaperized American girl and the rigid, old-fashioned, conservative still shockable and much shocked little society' — will need to be conveyed through conversation, description and incident. In the course of the presentation even the comparatively subtle scheme which the notebooks reveal becomes infinitely more complex. Consciousness is not only revealed rather than written about; it is presented with all the emotional force which careful attention to the nuances of language can provide. As incident follows incident, the ironic juxtaposition of contrasting scenes can gradually build up a complex awareness of the density of personality and of the complexity of the issues at stake. The skill of the writer may gradually reveal the implications of initial pretensions not through direct revelation but through the cumulative effect of speech and incident.

It is necessary, indeed, to insist on the precise form of the words used by a great writer, for there is nothing but the words to depend on. Any analysis of the finished drama for purposes of criticism offers but an abstract schematisation of the emotional and intellectual complexity of the original. Even ' "character" is merely the term by which the reader alludes to the pseudo-objective image he composes of his responses to an author's verbal arrangements,' as Mr C.H. Rickwood said in one of the best brief discussions of the nature of fiction I know of, though published over forty years ago. 'Only as precipitates from the memory are plot or character tangible; yet only in solution have either any emotive valency,' he continues. So important is this point about the precise nature of the language used for an understanding of the nature of literature and of the effects it can create that I propose to illustrate it by an examination of two versions of the 'same' scene (I shall argue that in fact they emerge as two quite different scenes with only the haziest of relationships between them) told in very different languages. In so far as language is a basic (perhaps *the* basic) tool for the revelation of consciousness of the social world both for literary artists and social scientists, this revelation of the importance of the precise implications of different linguistic expressions of the apparently 'same' social incident is essential to my theme.

Both versions seek to represent the scene after the killing of King Duncan by Macbeth. The Shakespearean version will be found in Act II, Scene 2, lines 44-63; the other is in the form of a strip cartoon; and I will briefly describe the visual impression and the revised words allotted to Macbeth and his wife. In the first frame Lady Macbeth is seen holding the daggers with her husband slightly behind her gazing, in what is meant to imply horrified silence, at his hands. Lady Macbeth says 'Then I must finish what you've left undone. Wash the filthy blood from your hands and quickly put on your night clothes in case someone comes.' In the second frame Macbeth is drying his hands on a towel with a bowl of water and a ewer in front of him. 'What is that loud knocking at the castle door? Who can be about at such an hour?' he asks. We are told that 'The knocking continues for several minutes. . . .' In the third frame Lady Macbeth is shown standing slightly above her husband on a staircase and holding aside a curtain to reveal him standing in a state of terror: 'I fixed everything,' she says, 'Come away now! The porter will answer the door. If we're called, it must appear we were aroused from slumber.'[5]

I would draw attention to two passages in each version, where clearly the one is intended to be a 'translation' of the other; and I will examine them in the light of the strip cartoon's claim to render 'All the thrills, terror and action of Shakespeare's great tragedy' as being 'here for your reading enjoyment. And the story is told in plain, easy-to-understand language.'

Let me begin by drawing attention to a small discrepancy. The strip says 'Wash that filthy blood from your hands . . .', whereas what Shakespeare originally wrote was: 'Go get some water/And wash this filthy witness from your hand.' Rhythmically the two statements are quite different, of course. This is the first thing that strikes the reader. The injunction 'Go get some water,' which might be thought redundant (how else would he wash?), accumulates imperatives which convey the tension of the moment, at once urgent and controlled − the very deliberateness of the phrasing suggests the latter (this is partly the function of '*this* filthy witness' in contrast to '*the* filthy blood' of the strip.) In other words, the emotional impact of the two sentences is very diverse. To that extent at least one is given a deeper insight into the behaviour of Lady Macbeth in the original than one is in the strip; to that extent, even in so small a detail, the 'action' is shown to be significantly different in the one from what it is in the other.

This point can be reinforced by further analysis. The strip uses the explicit word 'blood', whereas Shakespeare chose a metaphor 'witness'. The difference is significant. 'Witness' enriches the implications of the situation, as well as being more rhythmically telling in that it assists the intensity of the utterance. (Note the repetition of the 's' sound.) The blood is not merely blood; it is a testimony, which will reveal the crime if seen. Furthermore, it has associations with law courts and the resolution of crimes; it places the killing in its correct context of crime and punishment; it looks forward to Lady Macbeth's 'Out damned spot! out I say!' when indeed, in her imagination the blood becomes an undeletable testimony to guilt.

We note, indeed, that this element − at once psychological and social − of guilt and retribution is almost entirely omitted from the cartoon. The Shakespeare extract builds up a vivid picture of the inner consciousness of the two protagonists; the strip achieves little but a bare report of the incidents. For instance, in the latter there is no reference at all to 'great Neptune's ocean' and the consequent reddening of the 'multitudinous seas'. The action is the less meaningful for the omission. Rhythmically − and intellectually − the omitted passage reflects Macbeth's feeling of overwhelming guilt and expresses it in images of universal significance. This is not after all a private murder but one of the head of state; its repercussions will affect the journeyings of all who traverse the high seas or all who benefit from the ocean ways − all mankind indeed. The hyperbole at once fixes a state of mind and helps define a social repercussion: the sea is not a private but a universal symbol.

I could pursue the analysis further, but I have said enough to make the point I wish. If the action of the murder is conceived of not simply in terms of the actual act of sticking the dagger into the flesh of the sleeping king but includes the consciousness of the protagonists at the period of the deed, then what we have here, it is arguable, are two radically different murders. At the last, *as reported* (and we have nothing else to rely on) we are obliged to see the two actions as qualitatively different. There is no indication at all in the strip that Macbeth is suffering in any way from the pangs of guilt to the extent that he is. Even the picture of him looking at his hands could be interpreted at the level 'God, what a [physical] mess I'm in'. If we interpret it as anything more it is simply because we have read the Shakespearean original.

It is possible to generalise the point I am making by urging that one of the roles of literature lies in its amplification of, and precision about, states of consciousness which help to define social situations (which the murder of Duncan — as indeed, any murder — inevitably is). Now, of course, the creative writer is in a privileged position. He would appear to have total control over his creations; furthermore his craft is words. Where the former point is concerned, I have already, I hope, hinted that, in effect, his control is subject to certain checks and balances. He is subject to the need for inner coherence and verisimilitude. His characters, once charted, must remain consistent or change only to the extent that they may be said to have a potentiality for organic growth within them. His story, if he belongs to the tradition I have outlined, is likely to be geared to the requirements of 'typicality' — interpreted as relevance to a major area of human concern. At the same time, his theme is defined, not in terms of abstract thought or 'ideas', rationalistic abstractions which sum up an attitude or an orientation, but through the very medium of action itself. His aim is twofold: at once to reveal a truth (if he is a serious writer) and to excite an interest. Hence the core of his fable is normally a conflict, and the elements of his concoction must be geared to illumine not only the truth but also the dramatic situation. We are to be faced, not with an analysis of the phenomenon of 'newspaperization' and publicity — a social manifestation of considerable psychological and sociological interest — but a distillation of features of this phenomenon in terms of a conflict between two opposing attitudes towards it and of the 'real life' implications of such opposition for the characters in ways which may have little to do with the phenomenon itself. From the point of view of the investigator into the phenomenon of 'newspaperization', the mooted break up of the marriage plans in James's proposed story seems an irrelevance, except possibly marginally as an indication of the strength of feelings involved. But, in an era which so approves 'investigative journalism' this may reveal a neglected moral standpoint.

All this amounts to making the obvious point that a piece of literature is not the same as a social investigation. But my purpose, of course, is to show to what extent some study of the former can be of general assistance in the pursuit of the latter. Having drawn attention to some important features of the literary artist's undertaking, it is now necessary to look more closely at the role and practice of the social scientist, in order to see where there are any possible points of contact.

But I will need to begin with some meta-social science — with some analysis of the terms on which social investigations can proceed. We need to ask questions about the nature of social reality, seek the topography of the social world. Here I will find useful one of the most systematic attempts that has been made to clarify the nature of that intersubjectivity which is the basic stuff of our social intercourse, the work of Alfred Schutz. In his phenomenological studies of the complex nature of social interaction Schutz starts from Husserl's descriptive characterisation of what he called 'the world of the natural attitude' — the common-sense world, that is, in which we find ourselves from moment to moment in our daily lives. Schutz further elaborates this *Lebenswelt* and links it with a thoroughgoing examination of Max Weber's concept of *verstehen*, by which it is possible to seek an *interpretive understanding* of this social world. For, of course, Schutz's aim — like that of all social scientists — is consciousness, and the terms in which consciousness of others in the social world can be said to exist.

His attempt, then, is to define the nature of our consciousness of this common-sense world in terms of our human awareness of social action — 'social action' being defined in terms of behaviour to which a subjective meaning is attached on the part of the actor. For it is this subjective meaning which Schutz sees as the true *object* of the social scientist. The dilemma of the social scientist arises out of the fact that, in contrast to the natural scientist, he is forced to work at two levels of meaning, not one. The phenomenon investigated by the natural scientist has the meaning assigned to it which arises from human convention; it does not itself assign meaning to its own existence. But the social scientist is investigating a phenomenon which creates its own meaning independent of any meaning the scientist may choose to assign to it. The task for the social scientist arises out of the attempt to objectify, in accordance with good scientific principles, what already exist as subjective meaning-structures. The basic problem of the social sciences, then, is that of understanding what cannot be investigated by observation, what goes on in the minds of other people. Thus 'meaning' is at the core of the social scientist's problems, and the nature of *interpretive* understanding at the centre of his methodological puzzlement. It is to clarify how meaning can be assigned in the intersubjective world of everyday social life that Schutz devoted his first important work, *The Phenomenology of the Social World*.[6] A work of almost over-scrupulously careful analysis, it begins by investigating the nature of our personal consciousness, distinguishing between the moment by moment flow of sensation and action, and our awareness of meaning which arises out of the recognition, identification or reflection of this lived experience, by which it is lifted out of the stream of duration and made an object of contemplation. There is thus always an attribution of pastness in our awareness of meaning. Even our future plans must always be conceived in terms derived from the past — in the 'future perfect tense' as Schutz puts it.

Furthermore, motivation — what we intend — is crucial to what we mean by what we do: and Schutz distinguishes between two sorts of motivation — what he calls 'in-order-to' motive and 'because' motive. Motives which express themselves as ends to be achieved by the protagonist are called 'in-order-to' motives; motives which can be explained on the basis of the protagonist's background, environment or personal characteristics he refers to as 'because' motives. 'In-order-to' motives are those subjective formulations of the action by the actor which explain his future action as a manifestation of consciousness (his aims and purposes). The analysis of the objective conditions underlying 'because' motives is achieved only by a deliberate act of self-explication after the project has been formulated and the action completed. As, then, the project for a future plan belongs to the future perfect tense, the analysis of 'because' motives belongs to the pluperfect tense.

It is, of course, the analysis of intersubjective understanding that is of major interest to the social scientist. The starting point of the social sciences is the ordinary social world. Now we cannot, in general, expect to know other people as well as we know ourselves. The question is, how do we come to any knowledge of what other people mean by what they do, and of their 'in-order-to' motives? Clearly this will vary in accordance with our degree of personal contact with the other. Schutz distinguishes carefully between the sort of understanding which arises out of our face-to-face contact and that which can be gained of what he terms the 'world of contemporaries'. In what he refers to as the 'We-relationship', opportunities are afforded, for instance, of directly questioning the meaning of the other person. As we move from the 'We-relationship' to the 'They-relationship', so interpretation of the other's meaning becomes increasingly difficult and abstract. In many situations, indeed, it is only possible to understand subjective meanings from such evidences as we can muster. The world of contemporaries (like that of predecessors and successors) can only be known by indirect means. There is no possibility, in most cases, of direct grasp, through observing their involuntary actions, questioning them about their meanings. It is necessary to work by inference. In interpreting their activities, we resort to the creation of Ideal Types. And the use of Ideal Types always occurs when we pass from direct face-to-face social contact to indirect social experience; though in the process of creating them we draw on our experience of people in general.[7] Such Types indeed can be arranged on a scale of increasing anonymity. As the Type becomes more and more remote, so we are getting further and further away from the subjective meanings of the people we are concerned with. We make greater and greater use of typical objective meaning-contexts. Nevertheless, these typical objective meaning-contexts still constitute means by which we seek to question the subject, however anonymous. They will have a reference back to his action and motives for action; they still constitute a mode of confrontation, a questioning of the, by now, remote other; and his social actions, what he means, can only be understood in terms of his subjective meaning-structures, of greater or lesser anonymity. Such is the essential nature of the social world and of its mutual understanding.

The question now arises as to how we go about constructing these Ideal Types. The later work of Schutz is concerned with applying the insights of *The Phenomenology of the Social World* to working out a methodology for the social sciences. The basic problems should by now be clear, and can be briefly summarised. The object of the social scientist's concern is social behaviour. But social behaviour, unlike the behaviour of material particles, carries meaning for the participants and is controlled by their consciousness of this meaning. What we seek then, is the meaning of a meaning, not just a meaning: human beings do not simply behave – they themselves in some degree control that behaviour. The world is, in part, a construct of mind; how do we form a construct of a construct? In the first place, we must accept certain postulates about the nature of intersubjectivity in the social world. One of these is of such importance that I must spell it out at length. I shall refer to it as the 'democracy of shared perspectives'. What I see from 'here' and my fellow man sees from 'there' can, for common-sense purposes, be assumed to be interchangeable. Within the common-sense world it can be taken for granted that events and objects are intersubjectively available and more or less the same for ordinary perceivers – they possess what Schutz terms an 'again and again character' and are, 'basically homogeneous and repeatable'. Though Schutz grants that differently determined biographical standpoints imply that there will necessarily be a certain difference of subjective response, this is not likely to affect the common events of the real world – for such a world is one 'in which I assume that you are seeing the same table I am seeing.'[8] And, indeed, Schutz would seem to imply that subjective differences are purely matters of personal association and need not affect the process of typification which is an essential element in the creation of Ideal Types; for *'The typical and only the typical is homogeneous.'* As he puts it:

> the differences in perspectives originating in my and his unique
> biographical situations are irrelevant for the purpose at hand of
> either of us and that he and I, that 'We' assume that both of us have
> selected and interpreted the actually or potentially common objects
> and their features in an identical manner or at least an 'empirically
> identical' manner, namely, sufficient for all practical purposes.

This, then, is an essential postulate for the turning of ordinary social experience into the findings of social science; for social science must assume this world of typical intersubjectivity. Schutz further explains these 'common objects' in terms of the way of life considered to be 'the natural, the good, the right one by members of the in-group', 'typified knowledge of a highly socialised structure which supersedes the thought objects of my and my fellowman's private knowledge of the world as taken for granted.' And this leads him to consider that much of our knowledge is in fact socially derived – from friends, parents, teachers and the like: 'The typifying medium par excellence by which socially derived knowledge is transmitted is the vocabulary and the syntax of everyday language.' And he continues:[9]

> The vernacular of everyday life is primarily a language of named things and events, and any name includes a typification and generalization referring to the relevance system prevailing in the linguistic in-group which found the named thing significant enough to provide a separate term for it.

While he admits that 'knowledge has manifold degrees of clarity, distinctness, precision, and familiarity,' this would seem to involve largely the differing natures of personal expertise which characterises different members of the social world: 'I know whom and under what typical circumstances I have to consult as a "competent" doctor or lawyer.'

Even in the ordinary common-sense world of social intercourse, the 'subjective interpretation of meaning' by means of typification is a commonplace; we interpret our companions' behaviour in terms of a rationally assessed abstraction of typical possibilities projected from our past experience of similar or analogous situations. This process of typification provides the basis of the social scientist's procedure in his investigation into social activity and its motives and meanings:[10]

> By particular methodological devices . . . the social scientist replaces the thought objects of common-sense thought relating to unique events and occurrences by constructing a model of a sector of the social world within which merely those typified events occur that are relevant to the scientist's particular problem under scrutiny.

The situation he is observing is to him only of cognitive not practical interest; he looks at it 'with the same detached equanimity with which the natural scientist looks at the occurrences in his laboratory.' Furthermore, 'The scientific problem, once established, determines alone the structure of relevances.'[11] Guided by this system of relevances he proceeds in a way very similar to that of the non-scientific observer of the social scene, though his orientation and system of relevance is the problem in hand, not personal wishes and desires. He thus needs to posit an essentially rational world, one of rational acts and rational choices from rational motives. In this way he constructs typified actors for his consciously limited field of action. These Schutz terms 'homunculi': the social scientist[12]

observes certain facts and he constructs typical behaviour or course-of-action patterns from what he has observed. Thereupon he co-ordinates to these typical course-of-action pattern models of an ideal actor or actors, whom he imagines being gifted with consciousness. Yet it is a consciousness restricted so as to contain nothing but the elements relevant to the performing of the course-of-action patterns observed. He thus ascribes to this fictitious consciousness a set of typical notions, purposes, goals, which are assumed to be invariant in the specious consciousness of the imaginary actor-model. This homunculus or puppet is supposed to be interrelated in interaction patterns to other homunculi or puppets constructed in a similar way. Among these homunculi with which the social scientist populates his model of the social world of everyday life, sets of motives, goals, roles — in general, systems or relevances — are distributed in such a way as the scientific problems under scrutiny require.

These constructs are not, of course, arbitrary. They must be logically consistent in order to establish their objective validity; they must refer to typical possibilities of subjective action in relation to the observed action, and must therefore be adequate to the common-sense experience of social life and consistent with it.[13]

The rational course-of-action and personal types have to be constructed in such a way that an actor in the life world would perform the typified action if he had a perfectly clear and distinct knowledge of all the elements, and only of the elements, assumed by the social scientist as being relevant to this action and the constant tendency to use the most appropriate means assumed to be at his disposal for achieving the ends defined by the construct itself.

Now this begins to sound at least recognisably similar to the work of a novelist or playwright. It is true that these have differed among themselves in the way they have set about their business. James, as we have seen, started from a 'germ' of social action, a hint of a fable. But Turgenev always started with a character, to such an extent that he wrote out their biographies up to the start of his story. His aim, as he pointed out, was[14]

to show my people, to exhibit their relations with each other; for that is all my measure. If I watch them long enough, I see them *placed*, I see them engaged in this or that act, in this or that

37

difficulty. How they look and move and speak and behave, always in the setting I have found for them, is my account of them . . . .

The time, then, has come to make the attempt to work out similarities of procedure which will help to define in fairly precise ways the sort of assistance which the social scientist can expect to get from the literary artist; and, at the same time, insights of literary artists may serve as warning signals against placing too great a reliance on too rigid an interpretation of the *scientific* possibilities of social observation.

To begin with, they both move within the common-sense, unspecialised world of daily life – the world within which people read newspapers, commit crimes, feel guilt, go to work, make love. Both, out of this common-sense world, construct models which have reference to their specific aims; that is, the scientific – or artistic – problem, once established 'determines alone the structure of relevances.' Both, that is to say, construct independent worlds of interrelating human beings – 'homunculi' or 'characters' – as abstractions out of the real world. Furthermore, both construct actions which contain nothing but what is relevant to the course-of-action patterns under observation: they are equally concerned with the need for internal coherence and logical consistency. Both are totally in command of their puppets. Both may well start, as we have seen James doing, from a social situation which attracts their attention. In the process of *talking about* their creations, both strive for a certain typicality of behaviour. The social scientist does so because it is necessary for the nature of his scientific enterprise, the artist because it is essential to throw a certain air of plausibility over his action in order to appeal to the sympathies and understanding of his audience.

It is here, however, that the behaviour of the two may in some degree be said to divide. Up to now we can perhaps see that practice of the one might well assist that of the other: there is some similarity between the creation of characters and homunculi and familiarity with the one may well stimulate a wider perception in the setting up of the other. Yet a divergence does take place. For one thing, the social scientist is confined to an attempt to work out a range of possible typical reactions, for once these typifications have been stated, his creative task is largely over. He then employs these constructs as the terms in which he confronts the real world. For him, they exist only as means to further ends, and his concern is to get them 'right' so that the next stage of his procedure – the actual investigation – may also produce correct results. The aims and therefore the procedure of the artist are rather different; for, of course, to use Schutz's terminology, the 'in-order-to' motivations of the two are dissimilar. The main aim of the writer is to entertain in a rather austere sense of that word; and in order to do so he must demonstrate his characters in a particularity of circumstance which is foreign to the design of the scientist. The pull of the scientist, indeed, is towards generality, that of the writer towards particularity. I do not wish to exaggerate the tendency in either case. The orientation of the scientist will still be towards actions as committed by individual men; these will form part of the pattern of typifications which he projects. In the same way, the writer's orientation will be towards generality, in that he will want to give his fable some element of general application — 'typicality' in James's sense. He is communicating with a public world and needs to rely on public recognition. Nevertheless, the writer will disguise the generality of his creations by placing them in very specific situations and by giving their typicality a specific psychological and situational setting. What is at issue in the James story is not only two 'typical' responses to the social phenomenon of 'newspaperization' and publicity, but a whole series of circumambient circumstances, coherent indeed with the attitudes of the protagonists, but irrelevant, clearly, to the creation of 'homunculi'. Thus it is a girl's love affair which is at stake in the reactions to publicity; and the conflict which arises as well as the preamble to the clash, would be defined in terms of particular minutiae of behaviour and specificities of conversation. It is true that the incidents and the conversations would all be geared and the incidents all directed to illumine, in the last resort, the 'in-order-to' motives of the chief personalities. I must stress that art, like science, is an abstraction, and the selectivity of art is a selection geared, in the last resort, to the internal dynamics of the action — and that action, as I have made clear, ultimately has reference to the real, common-sense world.

I can put this another way. The exclusive aim of the scientist is to satisfy the intellect, that of the artist in part is to touch the feelings. Yet even here, we must be careful. The dichotomy of intellect and emotion is too easily accepted. As I have been at pains to emphasise elsewhere, they are rarely to be found in their pure state.[15] Certainly, a work of literature is not simply a howl of rage or a cry of delight; it makes an appeal to the intellect, and novels and prose plays make more appeal to the intellect, in general, than does poetry. It is not an accident that with the development of science, the prose novel has become the characteristic art literary form, and the verse drama, for instance, has almost completely disappeared. Nevertheless, the effect of incident and speech is at least partly emotional in orientation; they provide nuances of people in action that the typifying scientist necessarily misses. He never translates his notebooks into conversations, incidents, quarrels and the like. His homunculi interact — but only at the level relevant to the abstractions of intellect. They are there to be *talked about*, but never *presented*. Their love life does not exist —

except in an offshoot of Kinsey; certainly it has no relevance to 'newspaperization'.

Furthermore, in interaction patterns, the homunculi must illustrate the democracy of shared perspectives, which, as we have seen, is one of the basic assumptions of the scientist in his claim to interpretive understanding. Yet here, surely, we are brought up short; for I have just attempted to adduce literary evidence which may help us to see that the postulate of the democracy of shared perspectives constitutes a very doubtful assumption about the reality of the social world, to an extent indeed, that social scientists do not seem fully to appreciate.

I have tried to show how a happening in the real world — a murder — can, in two different expressions, take on a very different and complex meaning. One presentation gives the bare bones of the incidents; the other explores the meaning not only in terms of the actual killing (dagger, blood, etc.) but the reverberations of the killing in terms of guilt, judgment and the like. There is a profound difference, too, in *intensity* of reaction, in emotional response. It is arguable, I would have thought, that such discrepancies of meaning about an incident reflect real discrepancies between the abilities of people in the social world to apprehend meaning, to realise common-sense implications and significances. An appreciation of the possibilities of such discrepancies received confirmation in the words of a great literary artist when William Blake urged that 'A fool sees not the same tree that a wise man sees.' That 'table' which Schutz postulates as bearing similarity of meaning to different onlookers is more opaque to our vision than he suspected.

Let me make it clear that what are at stake are not matters of personal biography, subjective accretions which Schutz is prepared to recognise while urging their irrelevance to the process of typification. It is the table, the tree, the act of murder in themselves, as objective characteristics of the social world that are in question. An act of murder is a bloody deed and is likely to be messy in the performance; it is also socially an act inviting judgment, producing repercussions, creating tensions. It is reasonable to regard these as at least possible, if not inevitable, outcomes of the act, and we miss much of its social significance if we don't imaginatively apprehend these possibilities.[16]

'Imaginatively' — the word comes aptly to hand. 'Imagination' in the popular mind too often connotes fantasy, unreality. In fact, to the literary mind it points to the penetration of the real world — the common-sense world of the writer, be it remembered — by mind. Coleridge defined imagination as the 'coalescence of subject and object', by which he implied that into the simplest seeming 'datum' a constructing, forming activity from the mind entered. At the same time, of course, this formative activity is itself structured by what is there to be seen. 'Understanding' indeed, involves an interactive process between world and mind in terms of which mind, while controlled by what is there, may in some senses be said to create what it sees. Implicit is the Kantian notion of the relationship between percept and concept.

In social science investigations, the art of typification is, in the last resort, the responsibility of the scientist. As Schutz defines it, it assumes a shared world, one in which the objects of contemplation are viewed in abstraction as showing certain universally accepted qualities which fit in with the democracy of shared perspectives. The 'typicality' of the artist (to which Henry James alludes) provides the *starting-point* in the common-sense world of phenomena which we may be said all to accept, in which he probes the surface of things and shows their deeper implications, their ramifications in individual lives. Yet his 'individuals' are still abstractions, claiming something of the universality which is an essential postulate of the scientist. Though the aims of the two differ in ways which I have explored, they have a common purpose to the extent that they seek an understanding of a social world. The writer seeks it through imaginative penetration; the danger is that he will produce the idiosyncratic. The scientist seeks it through type-creation; the danger is that he will be content with the superficial because he is bound by the limits of common sense. Ultimately, of course, the literary artist knows that the common-sense world doesn't exist: it is simply a postulate which serves us in our less attentive moments. As soon as we begin to ask questions of any profundity, the trees and the tables alter their shapes and their contours and murder rises above the level of a bloody mess on the hands.

Of course it will be argued that it is just the idiosyncratic that the scientist must avoid. He is, after all, *qua* scientist, concerned with regularity, repeatability. It is possible that this is his Achilles heel — the attempt to induce uniformity where, in fact, often none such can exist. Yet it is reasonable to assume that some degree of repetition must take place — otherwise language, concepts, would never make sense. Furthermore, the literary artist too needs a repeatable world, at some level, in order to assume he will be understood. He, too, as we have seen, offers abstractions which yet seek to universalise their meaning.

What surely is at stake is the *plenitude* of understanding. I can express this best by urging that what social scientists too often demonstrate is imaginative poverty. The world is an order; even the social world demonstrates certain levels of repetition. But the common-sense world is too desiccated a one to form an adequate postulate for investigation. At the very least, the scientist's typifications — and they will be necessary — should be informed by the kind of imaginative insight that the literary artist brings to *his* view of typicality. The scientist will not, of course, be able to follow so far. His view of an action must be confined to the matter in hand and not pursue its further ramifications: he has a system of relevances to create, not a story to tell. But what is relevant may well be the richer and deeper if an imaginative projection into the lives of his homunculi takes place similar to that used by the artist in the creation of his characters. What is thought to be 'typical' in the last resort is the product of a *qualitative* decision on the part of the scientist; he will not serve the interests of his science if he assumes too readily an egalitarian democracy of shared perspectives. At the very least, he must be prepared to make articulate what in many minds is inchoate or unformed; though in doing so he will do nothing more than a great literary artist already performs.

So I would suggest that an awareness of literary practice and creativity can act as both a help and a warning to the social scientist. As one of the great sources of the subjective interpretation of meaning – through characterisation and the display of character in incident – it invites a *degree* of imitation. Admittedly, at the stage the artist begins to *present* rather than to talk about his characters, there is a split between the activities of the two. At the same time, there is also a proferred warning. Regularity and repeatability, though essential postulates of the scientist, yet offer some outrage to the complexity of the social world. They ignore, for one thing, differentiation of value between apparently similarly defined social situations because they ignore that the subjective interpretation of apparently objectively defined analogous situations may differ greatly. Typification in the social scientist's sense nearly always – except in the simplest cases – does some outrage to the complexity of individual response to the social world and individual understanding of it: not simply at the level of personal and idiosyncratic association – the irrelevances of memory, if one likes, which associate a personal reminiscence with an otherwise clearly defined objective situation, as a broken love affair may make a particular participation in a social gathering unduly poignant but in a way quite irrelevant to the meaning of the gathering – *but at the very centre of the meaning itself*.

Perhaps the warning is to seek as profound a definition as is possible within the techniques at the command of the social scientist: there will be a gain in complexity even if there is a corresponding difficulty in quantification. I will try to illustrate my point by comparing two studies of a social institution – the grammar school – made in recent years by social investigators. One, I am sure, is more orthodox in its sociological handling of the material, the other to my mind produces the richer – if less quantified – picture. From there I hope, too, that I will be able to draw further conclusions relating to the importance of literature to the scientist.

II

The two books are *Values and Involvement in a Grammar School* by Ronald King (1969) and *The Living Tradition* by Frances Stevens (1960). I propose to consider how they both study the values of the teachers in the schools they have investigated – and to confine myself to these sections. But first I must say a word about the approach and the procedures adopted by the authors.

Dr King investigated a single school situated in the London area. Dr Stevens drew on nineteen maintained grammar schools situated in various parts of the country. Dr King gives a clear account of his approach and stresses its empirical nature. In his choice of methods he is at pains to avoid any imputation of introducing personal valuations into the study; such an introduction would, in his opinion, make the study 'scientifically suspect'. He therefore goes to four books written by 'well-known protagonists of the grammar school' and obtains from them forty values, 'sometimes actual quotations from the texts, others ... slight paraphrases'. The teachers were asked to score them on a four-point scale; in addition, to choose five as being more important than the others and one as being the most important. The values were then ranked as a hierarchy, in accordance with the teachers' responses, and we are given the rank order. They were also asked to score sixty interests and activities of their pupils and the suitability of sixty-six television programmes, both on a five-point scale. I shall, however, confine my attention to the ranking of the values.

Dr Stevens investigated nineteen schools. She issued her teachers with a questionnaire, of which 126 were returned. In addition she carried out interviews with Heads and members of staff, who, in some cases wrote to her later. Where the staff were concerned these interviews were held both collectively and, in some cases, singly. Dr Stevens presents her findings in a section of her book called 'The Teacher Speaks'; Dr King has a chapter headed 'The Teachers'. Dr King produces his lists with a little general comment; he points to Professor Bernstein's distinction between the expressive and the instrumental functions of the school and points to the extent to which the higher ranking valuations seem to refer to the expressive order. He relates this finding to a brief analysis of his four authorities. This includes a short criticism of Dr Stevens:

As an objective study of the grammar school [her] investigations have certain methodological shortcomings in that they use data gained anecdotally, and not always very systematically. The investigations were conducted and are presented mainly as ancillaries to the author's opinions. Frances Stevens' view is not that of the objective investigator, but that of the educational practitioner, whose view-point is refracted through a cluster of essentially teacherly value-judgment and personal feelings . . . *The Living Tradition* is concerned with the 'ought' of the situation, rather than what 'is'.

As proof of this judgment, he quotes Dr Stevens's introductory remarks:[17]

This book was written as a test of my belief that at the present stage of our social development 'minority schools' must be preserved in the State-maintained system in order to allow for focussing of interest and the continuance of the right kind of tension.

I have quoted these remarks by Dr King at length because I am proposing to argue that his account of teachers' views is in certain respects at least much inferior to hers. Dr Stevens conveys indeed a fuller and more coherent − essentially a more meaningful − picture of what grammar school teachers are after − of their values, that is − than he does, even if we include their ranking of their pupils' interests and television choices. Nor do I think that her picture is any the less objective, though I appreciate that this is a matter for argument. The fact that she starts with an interest − which she frankly admits − in the preservation of the grammar school in no way can lead us to infer that she has presented the evidence unfairly in order to serve her ends. As the bad as well as the good features of the grammar school are presented I see no evidence whatsoever to indicate that what she reveals is other than a fair summary of the teachers' remarks. Her commentary is intended to elucidate the meaning and significance of what has been set down in the replies, as indeed, to a much briefer extent, does Dr King. Even the most 'objective' sociologist bears witness, by his choice of theme, to some assumptions about its value; and Max Weber himself allowed for assumptions of value in the choice of subject. A 'value-free' sociology is intended to imply that the evidence is sought and subsequently presented in all its ramifications, without any interference on ideological grounds.

Dr King, however, does point specifically to 'methodological shortcomings'; and as, in general, it seems to me that Dr Stevens's ways of building up her picture of values of grammar school teachers are superior to his, I want to examine the practices of both in rather more detail. My point will be that she produces a much fuller and clearer picture of what grammar schools see as the *meaning* of their jobs, and this in part at least because she has presented her teachers with a more coherent structure in terms of which they can think of themselves; and secondly because she has allowed them a much fuller expression of their attitudes and feelings, so that their subjective meaning-structures are correspondingly more fully and clearly revealed.

Let me begin by examining Dr King's forty values. His original listing is not given – only the final rank order; but I take it that the values as presented to the teachers are expressed as they are on this list. These, it must be said, constitute only a selection of what he could have gleaned from his four 'authorities'; for there are a number of values implicit or explicit in Dr Stevens's book which Dr King has not used. Why he has chosen some rather than others is not, however, apparent, though I would have thought that as soon as a selection was made, it would destroy his claim to objectivity: only *he* could have decided on the relevance of some rather than others; or if it was a matter of numbers, he must have made the arbitrary decision to limit his choice to forty.[18]

But the difficulty I find if I place myself in the position of one of the answering teachers is to decide what some of the statements put before me *mean*. Of course at a level this is perfectly clear; there is nothing obscure about any of the offerings. On the other hand, there is nothing precise about them either. The virtue which received the most votes was the exhortation 'To practise honesty and truthfulness.' It seems to me rather like asking people if they are against sin: one would expect a very positive answer in both cases ... if the question was taken seriously. My own reaction is 'Yes, of course, highly desirable. But in concrete cases, what does it *mean*?' What I am getting at can be clarified if we turn to a much fuller probing of these virtues in a questionnaire distributed to the pupils. From this even a young person would begin to see that the virtues of truthfulness and honesty raise much more complex issues than might be guessed from the unequivocal query put to the teachers. For instance, what does one do about the statements 'It is sometimes right to lie in order to spare someone's feelings' or 'It's sometimes kind to lie.' On ethical grounds it would certainly be possible to vote agreement with both statements, one moral principle (kindness to others) clearly conflicting with another (truthfulness). Having thus made the pupils think a little, it's not altogether surprising that they should end up rather less enthusiastic than their teachers for these virtues.

My point is that the two ways of seeking responses to these virtues – the difference, that is, between a straightforward list to the teachers and the more complex probing of the pupils – is likely to make the *meaning* in *concrete action* of these moral excellences somewhat different as between the two groups. Now, it is true that Dr King admits that it is difficult to make comparisons because 'there exist no scores [for the questionnaire to pupils] for a representative sample of adults which would enable useful comparisons to be made.' But in his later comparison of teachers' ideal-expectations of pupils' value-changes

45

with his suggestions as to what value-changes actually takes place (based on significant age trends in response to three specific items in his test of attitudes to honesty and truthfulness, one of which is the one quoted above, 'It is sometimes kind to lie'), he urges that the pupils 'tend to have less respect for these virtues,' and thus belie the hopes of the teachers. Now I cannot see that on the evidence Dr King has provided he has any right to make this suggestion, simply because it is reasonable to point out that the two parties were presented with two different meaning-structures which may well have affected the 'voting' on each side. The teachers were bluntly faced with the need to rate these clearly desirable virtues ('clearly' in accordance with the common assumptions of our present-day society) just as they stood. For the pupils they were placed in a context which made them appear much more morally equivocal, an equivocation which it would be quite reasonable to support on ethical grounds.

I have gone into this point at some length because it seems to me to illustrate some of the highly complex problems of meaning in social investigations – and meaning, with its attendant postulate of typification is, as we have noted, central to such investigations. I will now add a word on this question of typification, as it relates to Dr King and Dr Stevens's questionnaires.

Implicit in any questionnaire is some ideal-typification of the situation under review. Out of the flux of experience it concentrates attention on certain matters relevant to the issue at stake. A question is a form of categorisation; it strictly limits the attention. At the same time, it is an instrument of consciousness – its implicit demand of an answer necessitates a formulation and an articulation. Inherent in any questionnaire relating to any social role will be a view of that role, or its system of relevances and expectations.

Judged on this view of a questionnaire, Dr King's offerings to the teachers appear a curious hodge-podge. He does not tell us in what order the virtues were presented, but they certainly reveal some curious omissions when they are considered *en bloc*. The first thing that would strike most people about a teacher is that he is a person who teaches. Furthermore, in a grammar school he is usually a specialist teacher, restricting himself to one or two subjects. As the greater part of his school life is spent in this way, it would be reasonable to suppose that he thought it an activity of some importance, and that one of the virtues he would look for in his pupils would be their willingness to learn what he is teaching. It is surely true that there are teachers who think that chemistry, history, literature and the like are important, though it is also likely to be true that, in common with many other people, they would like to inflate what they are likely to achieve in more generalised terms than simply 'a knowledge of history', 'a knowledge of French', etc. They are likely, that is to say, to see their subjects as both ends in themselves and as instrumentalities to further ends — wide interests, moral behaviour and the like.

What is remarkable about Dr King's list is that it is so unspecific. The only normal school subject that is mentioned is 'music' and the only 'skill' games; a general 'respect for learning' is mentioned and general attitudes to work and books appear. Otherwise it would be difficult to tell that this was explicitly addressed to *teachers* and was concerned with their activities in a *school*.

Whatever shortcomings there may be in Dr Stevens's questionnaire, the questions explicitly relate to at least some typification of the work of a *teacher*. After a couple of questions designed to establish length of service, Dr Stevens plunges straight into subject teaching and the effects on it of public examinations. Questions on the sixth form and certain defined areas of school concern — uniform, school meals, etc. — follow. Whatever weaknesses and omissions the questionnaire may have, it springs from a clearly defined comprehension of the immediacies of the teacher's task, directing attention on the subject, the examinations and the pupils, as well as on certain important if rather more peripheral elements relevant to a school.

Dr Stevens, too, seems to have evoked much fuller responses than are possible under Dr King's voting system. Her teachers have clearly felt free to express themselves, in some cases at considerable length, with a clear gain in depth and explicitness. It may be argued that her ruminative commentary in presenting the teachers' comments gives some justification to Dr King's criticism — that the investigations 'are presented mainly as ancillaries to the author's opinions.' Nevertheless, it is arguable that the lengthy extracts which she quotes enable one to gain a much fuller insight into the teachers' views of the value and meaning of a grammar school education — both its strength and its drawbacks — than comes over from Dr King's investigation.

More important still, it is possible to see that what would appear to be social phenomena with a common significance in fact vary in meaning in some degree in the minds of different teachers. A question about how the grammar school should regard table manners evoked these two replies:[19]

The fact that this question can be asked illustrates the fact that teachers have become more and more general nursemaids, doing all kinds of jobs which must detract from our efficiency as teachers.

As I see it, one of the grammar school's aims is to develop a cultured manner. This includes speech, bearing, taste in clothes and table manners.

It is clear that for the former 'table manners' constitute a form of primitive 'training' covering the elementary decencies of life, whereas to the latter they constitute a much more important element in the total life-style of the developing child. The latter subscribes to a view of education which looks back to the courtliness of the Renaissance, and the education which was implicit in the notion of the courtier; by implication, the other interprets the teacher's job as a narrow one of intellectual training. Inherent in the two brief statements is a considerable clash of ideology and value. 'Table manners' reveals a quite different meaning for one from the other. Clearly, at certain levels, this would not very much matter: if it were a question of who would be willing to volunteer for dinner duties, the deeper clash of meaning would be irrelevant, except at the level of explanation which, in the context, might prove interesting but not germane to the issue at stake. But in so far as the social scientist is concerned with a deeper 'social meaning', the difference is significant. Such differences of meaning could only be gleaned by Dr Stevens's method of allowing much more opportunity for the display of subjective meaning-structures; they would not appear by Dr King's method at all. Furthermore, some interpretation of the phraseology is necessary – part of the meaning of the first extract arises from the contemptuous emphasis on 'nursemaids', and all the implications of the word.

III

I must now begin to sum up the nature of the argument I am putting forward in this paper, drawing attention to some of the factors of it which may so far have been implicit rather than explicit. A concern for social meaning within a common-sense world has been found to be the common factor in the activities of both the literary artist and the social scientist. Both rely, in their investigations into this social meaning, on some element of typicality; for the writer typicality is a starting-point at least, a recognisable world of behaviour intended to strike a chord in the mind of the reader, to promote a common understanding. In his elaboration of his theme he may display the ramifications of his 'action' in terms which would make them quite unacceptable to a social scientist, for he has a tale to tell as well as a social phenomenon to explore. His movement is towards particularity, demonstrating a characteristic of a society in its influence on the private lives and intimacies of his characters. Nevertheless, in the course of doing this, he will be forced to indicate at least some of the characteristics of the social phenomena under review – these, after all, are the consequences of a particular recognisable response to a phenomenon like newspaper publicity and to some extent must be accepted as part of its possible *meaning*. To this extent he can afford insights which may well be valuable to the social scientist who is concerned to investigate the social phenomenon of the newspaper, even if *his* interest is a more curtailed one of immediate consequences – 'in-order-to' motives and the like. There may therefore be said to be this direct link between the two. In so far as the literary artist is a great one, it may well be that he will reveal implications which could be hidden from a more commonplace investigation.

But the practice of literary criticism affords itself one of the most rigorous trainings in the elucidation of a particular type of human meaning – that implicit in language – it is possible to have. The literary writer gradually acquires an inwardness with forms of expression – through constant contact with the best and most highly wrought models – which is of the greatest importance in the interpretation of all sorts of linguistic expression. I am not suggesting that his word in this matter is definite or irrefutable – all literary judgments, as Dr Leavis was constantly at pains to emphasise, take the form of 'This is so, isn't it.' Nevertheless training in the study of the implications of language is likely to be better than no training: and as so much social investigation relies, even in its more 'objective' forms, on language, I can only consider such training to be a gain.

Indeed, it may well be that the sort of 'objectivity' that social science research can seek will ultimately turn out to be an objectivity nearer that of literature than that of science.[20] We have noted some of the drawbacks even to that sort of typification which those who stress the need for interpretive understanding as the basis of social science nevertheless would seem to land themselves in. The fact is that the social world only achieves limited objectivity; it is itself the product of the minds that go to make it up, and these minds differ in intensity, and penetrative power – 'a fool sees not the same tree that a wise man sees' etc. This is as true of those who are asked to rate a number of 'values' (linguistically expressed, be it noted) in rank order as of those who are asked to write miniature essays on relevant questions. My own guess, as an outsider admittedly, is that a great deal of current dissatisfaction with sociology and attendant disciplines arises from its claim to a degree of objectivity which, by the nature of its material, it cannot claim to have. True, the lower the level of phenomena which are under scrutiny, the less dispute about its meaning there is likely to be. Some agreed reactions to trees will be easier to collect and likely to be more objective than an attempt to measure highly intangible entities like values in relation to a social activity such as teaching.

Put another way, I would argue that Dr Stevens's attempt is the more successful of the two I have studied simply because in some respects it is more literary. As a matter of biographical interest, Dr Stevens is in fact an English specialist. Dr Stevens is not so free with her figures and her exposition – though she prints her statistical results in appendices; to that extent she may seem to be the less objective. It is true there are dangers in the ruminative nature of her exposition though my view is that she avoids most of them. Yet the fuller answers of her teachers (not forgetting the superior quality of the typifications implicit in her demand on their attention, i.e. her questionnaire) make the social meaning of a grammar school teacher's values much more complex and in that respect alone, likely to be 'truer'.

The fact is that good utterance affords the most potent insight we can have into meaning, psychological or social; and among the best utterances we have are those which have survived the years and centuries and come to be recognised as our literature. Furthermore, in the process of doing so they have achieved a sort of objectivity, and a typicality. It is true that different generations assign somewhat different meanings to acknowledged masterpieces; up to the eighteenth century *The Merchant of Venice*, for instance, and especially the character of Shylock, were interpreted in very different ways from what they are today. But these differences are not arbitrary; they receive a sanction in the ambiguities of the writing itself – is he just a figure of fun or is he the tragic figure we see him as today? The text can be read in both senses, and it is not simply the Nazi horror which makes it possible (if not obligatory) to play the part as a tragic one. The fact that these plays – and Shakespeare wrote much greater ones than *The Merchant of Venice* – endlessly exercise the interest and imaginations of people indicates that they achieve some universality of appeal, touch some common chord in humankind throughout the centuries. To that extent at least their ambiguity is controlled and their typicality assured.

Now clearly, social science cannot be written as if it is a novel. Too much of such writings could be irrelevant. Nevertheless, in so far as social science is concerned with the consciousness of men – and social institutions, *in the last resort*, only take their meaning from the way in which men conceive them and are prepared to accept them – it is arguable that the sort of typification which would best serve the social investigator would be that which sought the objectivity *and impersonality*[21] of the literary artist – the attempt to plumb the deeps within a framework of the familiar – rather than one which tried to reduce subjective meaning-structures to the lifeless states of physical phenomena. For this *must* offend against the complexity of the events he is concerned to plot. The other approach will, also, but it is arguable to a lesser degree. And what we can offer in social science may never be anything other than possibilities and probabilities, not certainties.

At the same time it has to be admitted that *ultimately* the essence of the literary experience is possibly antipathetic to that of the social scientist; for great literature constitutes an emanation of the aristocratic principle which conflicts with the postulation of 'shared perspectives' on the part of the social scientist. What the writer depicts is a world suffused with value — even a gesture, he realises, can be beautiful or crude. It is no accident that all the major literary figures of the twentieth century have been 'anti-democratic' — Conrad, Yeats, Eliot, James, D.H. Lawrence. Now, in his *Invitation to Sociology* P.L. Berger finds a social order in which the conventional social forms have broken down, a particularly apt field for the sociologist's attention — he thinks that notions of 'seeing through', 'looking behind' are concomitants of a sociological perspective. This could be expressed in another way by saying that only in a social order where the quantified seemed significant could sociology flourish — and this is necessarily one in which a measure of reductionism is acceptable, so that those forms of social behaviour with implications of 'more' or 'less' — their support to the notion of quality where, for instance, 'politeness' can be opposed to 'crudity' — will seem irrelevant.

One can put the matter this way. A civilisation based on a literary experience — as the Elizabethan was on the classical — can produce *Antony and Cleopatra*, with its multiple perspectives and its constant value interpretations of the protagonists and the nature of their relationship — 'gipsy's lust', 'lass unparallel'd'. Today, in our quantified society, with its neglect of qualitative differentiation, one has a feeling that the *affaire* would simply be subsumed under the statistics for extra-marital relationships.[22]

Chapter 3

Discovery methods

A class of school children is at work by the side of the Thames, under the direction of a teacher. Some are discovering evidences of tidal behaviour, others are examining examples of the local flora and fauna. Still others are digging in the mud by the side of the river, and are taking some of their findings to the teacher. Among their discoveries they find a piece of an old pipe and part of the jaw-bone of a horse. A small group is measuring the height of a nearside bridge with a piece of weighted string. There would seem to be evidence of much bustle and busyness. Then the scene changes and we are back in the classroom. Three of the findings are being discussed with a teacher – the leeches, the horse's jaw-bone and the piece of old pipe. We learn that the piece of old pipe is of historical interest, that the horse's jaw-bone will provide the stimulus for a group of children to learn about anatomy – and so on.

A discovery lesson is in progress: the children are exploring the environment under conditions of a very free discipline and are learning from what they find. The lesson of which I have given a very brief description is taken from a number of programmes televised a few years ago on the BBC intended to show how modern methods work and to recommend their adoption by teachers. The series was called *The Expanding Classroom*. Clearly, then, this is regarded as a good specimen of its type. Perhaps, then, we will be justified in asking one or two questions about it.

But first of all, it is important to examine the theoretical background to these new methods, for practice without theory is blind. In any case, what I intend here is a theoretical discussion of these methods. So-called 'discovery methods' do not constitute anything very new in the history of teaching. Socrates employs a recognisable form of such methods in the *Meno* when he enables a slave boy to solve a geometric problem 'though [I] simply ask him questions without teaching him.'

In effect, however, the whole modern theory of 'discovery methods' appears quite explicitly in Rousseau's *Emile* (1762); and they were actually made use of by a small number of 'progressive' eighteenth-century parents and teachers — men like Richard Edgeworth and David Williams. Indeed, I think that one of the best ways to begin a brief study of the advantages and limitations of such methods would be to examine the grounds which Rousseau adduces for their employment, for these have not changed so very extensively in the intervening 200 years. Naturally there have been modifications, but the advantage of a clearly expounded view of the theory which Rousseau gives us is that the arguments can be seen all of a piece. For one of the criticisms of the employment of these methods I would make is that many teachers, even among those who pursue them, do not understand them in their full ramifications, and hence are not in a position to apply them critically and in the contexts in which they are likely to function best. A study of their origins should aid this process. Perhaps, too, the realisation that the debate is at least 200 years old will take some of the steam out of the present controversy. This, then, is how I propose to proceed.

Before we even get this far, however, I would like to set these methods in their context in the history of education. In societies in which scientific and technical understanding is little advanced, the main job of such forms of education as exist lies in the handing on of the traditional wisdom, whether in the nature of some sacred text or texts or in that of a classical learning acceptable to the aristocratic or oligarchical rulers or social leaders. At the lower levels it is usually a matter of induction into traditional skills under domestic or semi-domestic conditions. In all cases, the teacher is the repository of the traditional knowledge, essentially an authority, and passes it on as largely unquestioned dogma. The aim, in brief, is the transmission and perpetuation of the culture.

With the coming of scientific and technical development, an important change is introduced into the world of the curriculum. The new knowledge which, in a few centuries, grows rapidly in prestige, is hypothetical, not certain. Though the interpretation of the sacred texts was subject to dispute their form was not; they manifested the indisputable body of necessary learning and had to be acquired, if necessary by rote methods. The basis of the new learning was sense-experience and induction from it; not only, philosophically, was the precise status of sense-experience in some doubt (a matter much debated in the eighteenth century), but refinement of observation was found to alter the nature of the laws induced. The certainty of the old knowledge was thus destroyed. Furthermore, men became interested in new questions — no longer ultimate ones of destiny and essence but secondary ones of 'how' and by what methods.

This is where Rousseau comes in. Despite his reputation as the exponent of 'feeling', the most cursory reading of *Emile* will indicate that he was, in fact, profoundly affected by the growing prestige of science during the eighteenth century. There are several important ways in which this is relevant to the rationale he finds for his discovery methods of education.

In the first place, he applies to the study of children's behaviour suggestions of observation which had for some time produced admirable results when applied to the natural world. In other words, he recommends – if he does not entirely initiate – with all the force of his literary persuasion the subordination of the curriculum (what is learnt) to what he regards as the inevitable, and therefore 'natural', stages of children's psychological development. He makes, indeed, great play throughout his book with this word 'natural', for he thought he had discovered laws of human development analogous to and as discernible as 'natural' laws in the behaviour of matter. And here he perpetrated an important error which has dogged the development of 'progressive' methods ever since. For what he seems to be asserting in some crucial and prominent statements he makes in *Emile* is that the human world of value and choice can be treated in the same sort of way as the morally neutral world of 'natural' (i.e. material) phenomena.

Let me hasten to add here immediately that there is another aspect of *Emile* in which it would seem, by implication, that Rousseau corrects this error. Unfortunately he never makes this explicit, to the ultimate confusion of the reader and of later theorists. Let me examine the extremely important consequences of this failure.

Rousseau often talks as if a child's mental development occurs spontaneously. He has, for instance, a famous theory of negative education: 'The mind should be left undisturbed till its faculties have developed.' The terminology of 'faculties' is out of date; nevertheless one sees what Rousseau is driving at, and the modern concept of 'readiness' applied to children's development constitutes only a more sophisticated form of Rousseau's rather naive statement. Children's tuition is supposed to await a developmental 'readiness' to proceed. Nevertheless the modern concept of 'readiness' has its ambiguities also. Are we awaiting a spontaneous act of a child's maturational processes signalled to a patiently attendant teacher? Or can 'readiness' – and should it be – induced? Clearly there are all sorts of learning (of a highly abstract nature, for instance) from which young children cannot profit. There are contexts, that is, in which negativity on the part of the teacher is desirable. But the best psychological opinion now sees in the notion of readiness a mixture of two factors – the maturational, based on genetic endowment combined with purely incidental and chance experience, and consciously induced learning situations by pedagogically competent persons (teachers). In other words, the pedagogical preparations of the teachers can play an important role in the 'readiness' of the child to undertake increasingly difficult learning tasks.

Now, at the beginning of the last paragraph but one I warned that Rousseau himself also wrote on occasions as if he, too, saw this point. Though he often speaks as if the job of the teacher is to leave the child alone and let him develop 'naturally' (i.e. at his own spontaneous pace), he is also capable of quite categoric statements such as 'You yourself [i.e. the teacher or tutor] must set the pattern he shall copy,' and the tutor is urged so to prepare the child's environment 'that nothing shall strike his eye but what is fit for his sight,'[1] with the surprising injunction: 'As soon as the child begins to take notice, what is shown him must be carefully chosen.'[2] This would seem to license the most authoritarian intervention; and yet there is a subtle distinction being made, the examination of which will take us further into the rationale of *discovery* methods as such.

The stress, indeed, is on preparing the child's surroundings, or on what is to be *shown* him. Direct verbal instruction would seem to be out. Indeed this suspicion is confirmed when Rousseau says: 'Give your scholar no verbal lessons; he should be taught by experience alone.' Now it is true that modern advocates of discovery and activity methods seem peculiarly suspicious of verbal exposition – instruction – as a pedagogic technique. 'Reception' learning, in the sense that content is presented to, rather than discovered by, the pupil has indeed in some circles been under so much of a cloud that an American psychologist, Dr David P. Ausubel, has found it necessary to devote a justificatory volume to *The Psychology of Meaningful Verbal Learning*. In this book he makes some of the most acute and cogent criticisms of a too exclusive reliance on discovery methods yet produced, and stresses the crucially important role which 'reception' learning can play even in the education of young children. Why, then, does Rousseau along with other, later progressives, so distrust verbal instruction? Here we may find some important clues as to the thinking behind the emphasis on discovery methods as constituting the 'one best way'.

Rousseau was, in part, reacting against the humanistic education which stemmed from the Renaissance and was so exclusively verbal, often necessitating a degree of word-sophistication which was beyond the capacity of some children to grasp. What resulted could be a meaningless rote learning: 'What is the use of inscribing on their brains a list of symbols which mean nothing to them?' he asks. A modern would applaud; children should show some capacity for understanding what they are having to learn, otherwise it becomes meaningless doggerel to them. Instruction has come to seem a dirty word, because too often in the past children have received instruction without comprehension. The principle would seem unassailable.

Yet there are several points to be made. We need not go as far as Professor Oakeshott when he asserts that what characterises what is taught in school is that it has the quality 'of being able to be learned without necessarily being understood'; yet we can see that to lay exclusive emphasis on 'understanding' would involve some pretty drastic restrictions on curriculum. Quite young children are capable of tackling elementary Latin; they can 'understand' the meaning of sentences like 'Balbus murum aedificat.' But they are incapable of understanding the point of seeking such understanding, for the answer exists in terms of a need for cultural continuity and the meaning of such a notion they cannot even conceive. Again, many children quite early are capable of following and understanding something of a Shakespeare play, but their understanding will necessarily be a limited one.

But even if we accept the idea that 'understanding' is a crucial test of the validity of a curriculum or of a stage in a syllabus, there is no reason why such understanding should not be promoted by verbal exposition. The fact that instruction in the past has sometimes induced purely rote learning is no reason why it should always do so. I shall return to this point later.

The truth of the matter is that Rousseau — and some moderns — has a very limited view of the power and range of language. He seems to think that words always have something to which they refer and that unless the thing to which the word refers has been 'experienced', they simply constitute meaningless noises to children. This is not true; children are capable of getting considerable joy out of uses of words which nevertheless, in his sense, they cannot be said to 'understand' — an extreme form of this would be their enjoyment of nonsense words. Poetic statement, too, does not always invite complete understanding — as T.S. Eliot pointed out.

Now the source of Rousseau's error is comparatively simple. It springs from his belief, which he inherited from Locke, that the sole origin of human knowledge is to be found in immediate sense-experience of 'things' and objects external to the human being (and reflection on this experience). 'Our first teachers in natural philosophy,' Rousseau asserts, 'are our feet, hands and eyes'[3] (in other words, our sense-experiences and observations), and, he insists, 'experience precedes instruction.' Again, we see the scientific orientation of Rousseau's outlook. Hence the modern emphasis, which forms part of the rationale of discovery methods, on the need to afford opportunities to children for a wide variety of experiences; and, of course, there is something in it. But even here we have to be careful. For, of course, the notion that the child has *experiences* implies that the child achieves some degree of consciousness about what is happening around him. But consciousness isn't something that just happens to a child: it has to be sought and the child must himself bring something with him if the 'experience' is to be in any way meaningful. Perhaps an example may make this clearer.

I am technically quite inept, and I rely on the good services of mechanics if anything goes wrong with my car, for indeed I know practically nothing about its functioning. Let us say I suffer a breakdown in a wild and desolate spot. I raise the bonnet and face the engine. I see it, I touch it, I even listen to it. But because I have no idea of the meaning of what I see, my 'experience' is null and void, and the car remains stationary.

The fact is that the mind needs to bring to the experience a set of relevant concepts in terms of which the 'experience' warrants the term at all. Consciousness that an experience is being undergone only arises if the child has at his disposal a set of mental tools which enables him to order the bewildering mass of impressions in the external world in some meaningful way. It's no good setting children free in a field and asking them to 'experience' nature; they can only experience what they can already recognise. It may be that they will ask questions about some of the things they can already identify, or even on occasions point to something easily noticeable and ask 'what's that?' But even here this will only happen because they will already have learnt in a rough and ready sort of way to distinguish certain shapes and objects as having significance. Children from primitive peoples who have never seen a moving film before are unable to see anything significant on the screen because they have not learnt to distinguish two-dimensional moving figures and objects into discrete meaningful shapes having some relevance to the real world of people and things.

Now this raises the most fundamental issues concerning the sort of learning structures which are implicit in discovery education. By learning structures I refer to two things: I refer to the structures implicit in the environment within which the child makes his discoveries; and I refer to the mental structures of relevant concepts which the child brings to the environment with which he is being presented. For here I believe we are at the heart of some of the difficulties which arise in the use of discovery techniques.

Let me begin to tease out these vitally important points by taking an example once more from Rousseau. Rousseau wants in effect to turn Emile into a little primitive scientist. In the early stages he encourages a wide range of haphazard sensory occurrences:[4]

He wants to touch and handle everything; do not check these movements which teach him invaluable lessons. Thus he learns to perceive the heat, cold, hardness, softness, weight, or lightness of bodies, to judge their size and shape and all their physical properties, by looking, feeling, listening, and above all, by comparing sight and touch, by judging with the eye what sensation they would cause to his hand.

Susan Isaacs used precisely the same informal techniques with very young children at the Malting House School in the 1920s, and such ideas form an important aspect of informal play techniques in modern infant schools. But of course this haphazard sort of learning cannot go on for very long – or should not. I believe that the key to the whole controversy about discovery methods arises out of a quarrel – largely implicit rather than explicit – about the precise amount of structure which is to be introduced by the school into children's learning situations.

Under the old formal system the teacher presented material structured in accordance with convention or with such personal views on the matter as he might have. He was, as I have indicated, concerned to transmit the accepted, and the children absorbed and if necessary regurgitated (in 'tests' or examinations) what they had acquired. The disciplines involved were subjects which had gradually been added to the curriculum and which were thought to constitute what a broadly educated man needed to know. The treatment of these subjects at elementary level was often quite unsophisticated, usually constituting little more than lists of facts which those with good memories acquired without any understanding of relevance and, indeed, without having in any meaningful sense been initiated into the disciplines concerned. Thus, as I have said, instruction, because it was bad instruction, fell into disrepute. Nevertheless, the structure, even if it was an inadequate structure (conceived in terms of the real meaning of disciplines), was clear and unequivocal. History, for instance, was the dates of the kings and queens of England – it was often as simple as that.

The new methods have sought to harness the informal curiosity of children of the sort Rousseau describes and use it for pedagogic purposes. (As I shall point out later, motivation has been a key factor in the new movement.) Unfortunately teachers have been confused as to how or when informality should be turned into formality – when, indeed, structure should be involved and even imposed, when the demands of the school as an instrument of structured learning should replace the haphazard if stimulating early learning experiences.

Here, then, we see the reason for Rousseau's dilemma. He wants Emile to learn informally at his own pace – so he urges the teacher to do nothing. At the same time, he realises the need for order in the development of subject-matter – so he stresses the need for experiences to be presented to the child 'in fitting order'. Let us see how he copes with this dilemma in helping Emile to acquire some knowledge of science.

'Let him not be taught science, let him discover it,'[5] and Rousseau involves the child in a series of observational situations when important scientific principles may be involved – magnetism, gravity and the like. He admits that young children cannot go far in the study of purely theoretical science, but he urges:[6]

> take care that all their experiments are connected together by some
> chain of reasoning, so that they may follow an orderly sequence
> in the mind, and may be recalled at need; for it is very difficult to
> remember isolated facts or arguments, when there is no cue for their
> recall.

How far here are we from the injunctions of negative education! Yet too many modern teachers, in the euphoria of the new-found freedoms, have neglected the structural aspects, possibly partly because there are times when the orderly development of subject-matter can best be furthered by intelligent and relevant formal exposition and explanation.

Let me now illustrate the point from the account of a discovery lesson I gave at the beginning of this chapter. The children have gone down to the side of the river in order to glean 'experiences' on an informal basis. They make a number of observations and bring back with them a heterogeneous collection of articles – some leeches in a bottle, a jaw-bone of a horse, a piece of an old pipe. The leeches form part and parcel of the natural life of the riverside, and, though the river as a phenomenon together with its attendant plant and biological life does not constitute a conventional 'subject' in itself – it involves geographical, botanical, biological studies among others – it is sufficient of an entity as an identifiable element in the environment to make it, in all its heterogeneity, a reasonable object of study, especially for young children. But the jaw-bone of the horse and the piece of old pipe are not part of the natural environment of the river: they are there purely by accident; they could as easily have been found on a piece of waste ground. They have no *structural* relationship to the river. Yet they too are treated as grist to the mill.

Now the danger of this sort of treatment is that it fosters what might be termed a magpie curriculum. Anything constitutes an experience and the children are encouraged to branch out into any and every direction which happens to be justified by the chance contiguity of objects. History, biology, anatomy jostle side by side, and children are persuaded to start after any hare that crosses their path, or that can arouse a temporary ebullition of 'interest' – and children's interests are often very temporary. (This is an important point to remember.)

But, the reply comes, this *is* life. Life doesn't parcel itself up into those neat 'academic' subjects (often regarded pejoratively by progressives) which the old-fashioned school timetable foisted on a lot of uninterested children. This is an education for life, not for the groves of academe, and children should be made to realise that the ordinary environment has its excitement and its interest. Now, there is a point here. A large number of children are not what is referred to as academically minded, and they (and indeed all children) do need to be shown on occasions that the immediate world does have its excitement and interest. We do need to do something in schools to counter the awful boredom which seems to engulf so many adolescents and makes them easy victims for the factitious excitement of the pop world. So it is right and proper that on occasions informal forays into the out-of-school environment should be made, and some of its riches and opportunities made manifest. Nevertheless, there is a law of diminishing returns at work here. For one thing, Rousseau is right: it is very difficult to remember isolated facts or arguments. Really to enjoy some aspect of the environment necessitates learning to recognise certain features — the architecture of cities and towns, insect life in field and hedgerow, to take two random examples — and really to pursue some such study in depth, so that experiences within the chosen field become genuinely meaningful. And as soon as one speaks of depth, of course, one implies a structure of conventions and concepts which a child must be helped to conquer in some sort of logical order. And this is just what the school is for. Bad academic teaching in the past has made some people suspicious of the academic, as if all it involved was the dull and the stultifying. But, in fact, academic subjects, so called, have evolved as they have simply because they have proved to be the most economical and lucid ways of handling the undifferentiated mass of phenomena we experience in the natural and social worlds around us or in the internal life of our feelings and emotions. That these subjects don't always reveal themselves in this way is due more to bad teaching based on imperfect comprehension of the potentialities of academic subject material than to deficiencies in the material itself.

In any case, there is an element of the absurd in Rousseau's injunction: 'Let him not be taught science, let him discover it.' Literally followed, this would be to throw away our human heritage, what, indeed, specifically makes us human: our ability to build on the findings of others. The notion that a child must follow through all the stages of human development under the steam of his own capacity to discover what his predecessors have already found out, is ridiculous. It is part of our human ability to be able to package, in assimilable form, information (concepts and relevant facts) which children can then digest at a rate which the original discoverers would have found astonishing. As we already have the structures, the job of the school is to find the best way of presenting them – and by 'best' I mean also the most economical.

This is why the notion of informality and that of school do not finally mix. It is precisely the purpose in setting up such separate and expensive institutions to enable learning to take place that they shall introduce coherence and order where none previously existed. There is, for instance, a cliché that teachers in junior schools often use – they refer to the 'family' atmosphere of the school. Now this is harmless when all it is intended to imply, as is often the case, is that relationships between the children and the teachers are reasonably kind and courteous – though it is a sentimentality to think that families always exist in these terms. But when it is implied that the same sorts of informality which reign in family life should also characterise the school, then the time has come to call a halt, and to indicate that, as often happens, a metaphor is usurping the job of clear thinking. It is precisely one of the characteristics of a school that it is *not* the same as a family – the nature of its relationships and its purposes is quite different. To suggest that the school should simply afford the same sort of informal experience to a child that a good parent would do – by taking him here and there to places which he will enjoy – is to mistake the purpose of setting up the school as a quite separate institution with a specially trained personnel to run it. A teacher is not simply a substitute mum or dad.

The suggestion, however, is often made that these discovery methods, where the child is set loose to explore an environment in a way which is too reminiscent of informal home circumstances nevertheless constitute a more *natural* way in which children can learn. Here again we ought to be on our guard. The word 'natural' is an extremely dangerous one, with many hidden traps for the unwary. It can mean 'natural' to human beings (in line with human 'nature') or it can imply some imagined transcendent principle in line with the supposedly beneficent workings of the non-human 'natural' world. In its latter use it tends to degenerate into a vaguely meaningless word implying general approval, as if in line with some ill-defined norm. It is, therefore, to be eschewed. If it is used in the former sense, it grossly misinterprets the nature of the human situation; for what characterises human beings is precisely their capacity for the rational determination of efficient means to accepted ends. Learning, then, becomes a matter of rationally determined methods, not a 'natural' process analogous to the habit-acquiring of the birds and animals; and it is part of human nature that it should be so. Rousseau, of course, creates great confusion over his appeal to 'nature' as a constant norm, and he must take some of the blame for the subsequent highly ambiguous usage of the term.

Yet there is a form of what might be referred to as 'natural' development where the word can — and has — served a useful purpose. It is undoubtedly true, as Rousseau, as we have seen, insists, that children have to pass through certain stages of development; and Rousseau's guesses as to what they are were remarkably acute for their time. He realised, for instance, as will have been implicit in much of the foregoing discussion of his ideas, that young children learn a great deal through the concrete, and from direct sensory experience. This has been largely confirmed by the work of the greatest of modern child psychologists, Jean Piaget. Piaget, indeed, terms the age of the junior school child as the stage of 'concrete operations'. Here, then, surely is a bedrock argument in favour of discovery methods, with their emphasis on bringing children face to face with the environment, and learning from it in concrete experience.

Again, however, we have to be careful. We are still faced with the necessity of children having to acquire the concepts necessary to make sense of this environment. It is important to realise that Piaget does not justify discovery methods as such. In any case, he is not (contrary to popular opinion on the subject) a learning-theorist. He says, as Professor Foss has pointed out, 'very little about the learning process. Piaget's enormous contribution has been ... in demonstrating how a child's *thinking* differs from that of an intelligent adult and how the child shows changes in *capacity* for solving problems needing certain concepts.'[7] It is quite wrong to think, therefore, that Piaget's findings in any way *validate* discovery methods. Clearly he implies that some form of concrete actuality is extremely important in children's learning; but he does not validate any particular method of presenting it. It would be perfectly possible for anyone drawing on Piagetian findings to introduce illustrative concrete apparatus of some sort into what would otherwise count as a perfectly formal lesson, dependent on teacher demonstration and instruction.

Then again, the Piagetian stages must not be regarded as rigid demarcations indicating the inflexible ability of all children to cope with certain sorts of learning at appropriate ages, as Susan Isaacs pointed out many years ago. Children do, in fact, manifest wide differences in developmental sophistication: some barely ever emerge from the stage of concrete operations; others enter on the stage of formal operations (implying the ability to handle certain sorts of abstractions) at a remarkably early age. It is these very bright children who often show considerable boredom with the leisurely informal pace of discovery methods — who yearn in fact to be *told* the answers to the questions they are asking because the answers will enable them to rush on to the next step in their eager intellectual inquiry. If discovery methods are used with these, they should be of the much more tightly structured type that Socrates used with the slave boy, when he led him from stage to stage by carefully framed questions — and indeed, the Socratic question is one of the best techniques by which a teacher can enable a child to make a discovery on his own. But, of course, it needs to be a very precise question, put by a teacher who knows exactly where he is going.

The point then that arises out of all this is, I hope, that these discovery methods constitute an important but limited addition to the vocabulary of teaching. They are probably particularly useful for arousing initial *interest* — their function as motivators should not be underestimated — and, with a child population many of whom are uninterested in school, this is not a factor to be despised. Furthermore, they can introduce children to a range of possibilities well beyond that of the old formal methods — they can make the world seem a more interesting place. Again, they help children to learn how to learn, without always having a teacher standing over them demanding a set piece in a set time. Children learn to rely on their own initiative to find out things, look up in books, etc.

But this enthusiastic picture needs to be curbed by a careful and thorough understanding on the part of the teachers as to exactly what they are aiming to accomplish, otherwise all the children acquire are a set of bits and pieces, orts and greasy relics, soon forgotten if ever really appreciated. The essence of their successful usage lies in their taking their place in a definite pedagogic scheme designed to aid initiation into complex learning structures which the teacher should have at his full command. To put it bluntly, he must work out for himself where he is going. There is a certain amount of research on discovery methods — *and it can be said quite categorically that the superiority of discovery methods cannot at present be justified on grounds of empirical research.*[8] Therefore, the teacher must rely on his own experience of what is effective and not allow himself to be bullied by dogmatists for the new order. He must certainly learn that the term 'discovery methods' covers a number of different sorts of 'discovery' processes — from the free environmental investigation implied in some of the early observational scientific studies to the carefully structured question-and-answer techniques implied in logical subject-matter, with its often carefully designed structural apparatus (e.g. Cuisenaire rods or Dienes blocks), provided to lead from one step to another. He must know that 'discovery' can and should be made from books — but that their use needs careful practice and a *trained* ability to glean relevant material from their contents. He should realise that in some subjects — such as literature — the main emphasis will still remain on his own personal charisma, on his ability to read well and feelingly in a class situation, for instance; and indeed that his power to excite interest and attention will always be fundamental. He will need to remember that instruction and planned repetitive work will still have vital roles to play, so that processes can be thoroughly explained, grasped and internalised by practice. He will even on occasions find that rote learning has a part to play – in the learning of spellings and tables, for instance. The point is that 'discovery methods' need to be collated with carefully presented and meaningful but quite formal instruction; and that the effectiveness of the Socratic question depends on his pedagogic skill and not on some spontaneous inner ripening on the part of the child.

There is, in fact, no one way. Subject-matter differs enormously in nature and demands quite different sorts of pedagogic devices for its efficient transmission. And effective learning *is* the most important function of the school – the only institution in our society explicitly set up for such a purpose – and if it is not accomplished there it will not be accomplished anywhere else. Used competently, with an awareness of their place in the general armoury of tools at the teacher's disposal, these new (not so new, as we have seen) methods have a great deal to offer. Used incompetently, as a gimmick or a fashion, they are probably more disastrous to learning than an exclusive reliance on the old formal methods. At least these took the business of learning seriously and made it seem an important matter; but these methods, with their permissive atmosphere, in the hands of an incompetent teacher are enervating and time wasting and can induce a lethargy of response more destructive than the soul's attention paid to the wrong thing.

Chapter 4

The idea of a liberal education

At the heart of the age-long controversy over the nature of liberal education, there has existed an uncertainty, an ambiguity. The most common way of speaking about liberal education today is that it involves the pursuit of 'knowledge for its own sake'; and something of the ambiguity which I detect in our handling of the concept can, I think, be glimpsed in the oddity of this phrase.

Odd it certainly is. When we speak of doing something for the sake of someone else, we usually imply that our action will somehow benefit the other person. A relationship, a reciprocity even, is indicated. 'I did this for the sake of my friend' or 'for his sake' implies a relationship between the two persons involved. Certainly, the 'friend' is affected; my action is oriented in his direction; what I do is done out of regard or consideration for him, it has him in mind, its nature is controlled by my understanding of his wants, needs and desires. Where, then, there is another person involved, the implied effect of my behaviour on him seems to be quite clear.

At the same time, I too am affected: if my action is oriented towards another, it reflects back on me; what I do is also controlled, and I choose what to do in a particular situation out of a range of possible actions *because* of my appreciation of the requirements of my partner; my behaviour, too, is structured by the relationship; my action reflects back on me as well as on to him.

Now when we say that we do something 'for the sake of understanding', or pursue 'knowledge for its own sake' ('for the sake of itself', understood), the situation is more puzzling, though basically it demonstrates the same reciprocity. If we take the latter phrase first ('knowledge for its own sake' or 'knowledge for the sake of itself'), it is difficult to see how my activities could affect knowledge ('itself') as

65

such. And yet clearly, there is a relationship implied between me and the knowledge. It appears, indeed, that there are two possible ways of looking at the meaning of the sentence. In the first place, it may be said to reflect back on the subject of the sentence, so that the sentence 'I pursued knowledge for its own sake' tells something about me in my enthusiasm for knowledge; it reports on the conditions under which I pursued knowledge, just as my actions previously were controlled out of consideration for my friend. But it also tells us something about the nature of the knowledge which I have been pursuing: it is knowledge whose *raison d'être* is to be found within itself, it is the sort of knowledge which can be sought after for the sake of what is in it, with no further relationship suggested other than with what is contained within the knowledge. Thus, though the knowledge is not *affected* by my behaviour (as my friend is), it is to some extent *defined*.

The point of all this is that if we define liberal education, loosely, as the pursuit of knowledge for its own sake (as is often the case), we may be saying something about the knowledge, and we may also be saying something about the pursuer, about *his* attitude to the learning he is seeking. I believe it is because we have not always been very clear in our minds as to which element in the relationship between individual and knowledge is being stressed that some of the confusion concerning the use of the concept has arisen.

This confusion can be illustrated admirably from a close examination of one of the classic expositions of the idea of a liberal education, that in Aristotle's *Politics*.[1] In Book 8, Aristotle turns his attention to the education of youth. He considers that education should be public and the same for all; for 'the citizen should be moulded to suit the form of government under which he lives'. Therefore education should be regulated by law and be an affair of the state. He then goes on to decide the form of this education, commenting on the current lack of agreement as to what should be taught. He admits the need to teach children 'those useful things which are really necessary,' but, he continues, 'not all things'. He then proceeds to divide occupations into two categories: 'for occupations are divided into liberal and illiberal; and to young children should be imparted only such kinds of knowledge as will be useful to them without vulgarising them.'

It is clear, then, that Aristotle sees that occupations are divisible, *in themselves*, into two categories, liberal and illiberal ones; and he goes on to a small extent to define the latter: 'we call those arts vulgar which tend to deform the body, and likewise all paid employment, for they absorb and degrade the mind.' This is not very precise, but it does point to a categorisation of liberal education in terms of the disciplines involved. Some pursuits seem to be inherently liberal. But he then continues by pointing to another criterion in terms of which an occupation may be considered liberal or illiberal. Here it depends on the attitude of the pupil. Thus some 'liberal' arts are acceptable provided we don't pursue them too avidly:

> There are also some liberal arts quite proper for a freeman to acquire, but only in a certain degree, and if he attend to them too closely, in order to attain perfection in them, the same evil effects will follow.

Again, the purpose for which a person pursues learning is also relevant:

> The object also which a man sets before him makes a great difference; if he does or learns anything for his own sake or for the sake of his friends, or with a view to excellence, the action will not appear illiberal; but if done for the sake of others, the very same action will be thought menial and servile.

Here, then, liberal education is defined in terms of the seriousness of the purpose the pupil has in mind in pursuing knowledge. Such education is, then, not only a matter of coming to grips with certain specific disciplines or areas of knowledge; the psychological attitude of the pupil is also relevant in deciding what is to be regarded as truly 'liberal'.

Now, it must be made clear that, in the original decision as to how to categorise occupations as liberal or illiberal, a social factor of great importance was involved. What Aristotle was defining was an education for free citizens only: an education, if you like, for free men – and to make men free. And from the ranks of citizenship slaves and all members of the trading and producing classes were excluded: 'Certainly,' he proclaimed, 'the good man and the statesman and the good citizen ought not to learn the crafts of inferiors except for their own occasional use.' And it is in this sense of class exclusiveness that we detect the reason why he considers that those who pursue a liberal education should not attend too closely to any specific discipline and should not seek technical perfection in it. His aim was much more nearly the production of what came to be known as the amateur gentleman than it was that of the professional expert. Indeed, to seek too concentrated an expertise is explicitly excluded – because such concentration on a narrow field blinds to other possibilities. Thus the idea of liberal education was opposed to the notion of specialisation. The Spartans are criticised because they brutalise their children with laborious exercises: for, in truth, 'as we have often repeated, education should not be exclusively directed to this or to any other single end.' To make children useful to the state in one quality only was to vulgarise them.

This is linked with Aristotle's stress on the importance of leisure: 'the first principle of all human action is leisure,' for 'leisure is better than occupation.' The link with liberal education is made quite explicitly: 'It is clear . . . that there are branches of learning and education which we must study with a view to the enjoyment of leisure, and these are to be valued for their own sake.' A little later, 'liberal' is linked with the concept 'noble': 'It is evident . . . that there is a sort of education in which parents should train their sons, not as being useful and necessary, but because it is liberal or noble.'

This traditional classic exposition of the case for liberal education is concerned with the production of a certain type of human being within a specific set of social conditions. It is because of this that one can perhaps see how the confusion over the implications of the concept has arisen: is it certain types of knowledge or a certain attitude of mind which is crucial to its meaning? We note that the knowledge is restricted in scope, defined in relation to certain approved types of social activity. On the other hand, the approved activities themselves are to be conducted in a certain way, without intensity, carrying with them, shall we say, a certain social tone. The matter and the *manner* are both relevant, and seem equally to be involved before it is correct to employ the concept of liberal education.

Only if this is assumed does the subsequent discussion on the educational value of music seem to make sense. It is decided that music is to constitute an important part of education because it has qualities relevant to the 'tone' of leisure, for it provides 'recreation'. For it to do so, it must be pursued in the right spirit of amateurishness: so

> the right measure will be attained if students of music stop short of the arts which are practised in professional contests, and do not seek to acquire those fantastic marvels of execution which are now the fashion in such contests, and from these have passed into education.

Virtuosity is not the aim.

But it is also true that the quality of that leisure takes its content from the nature of the music chosen; rhythm and melody provide imitations of important aspects of moral character. Hence it is concluded that 'music has a power of forming the character, and should therefore be introduced into the education of the young.' It exercises a formative power over the soul and educates the young to reality.

The introduction of the concepts of the soul and of reality remind us that the Greek doctrine of liberal education was sustained by certain philosophical and metaphysical views, a point made in an essay by Professor Hirst.[2] The end of education in classical Greek times was the formation of the perfect citizen, because it was through the city state that the Greeks realised themselves. Now the fully developed political sense of the great Greek philosophers involved, as a necessary and essential element in the right ordering of the state, the notion of hier-archy: some were born to rule, others to be ruled. The hierarchy of gold, silver and iron members of the community in Plato, for instance, illustrates my meaning. And the notion of hierarchy invaded the developmental aspect of education, its teleology. The attainment of reason was, in man, 'the end towards which nature strives,' but this was only attained as a result of a natural and hierarchical progression: the care of the body preceded that of the soul, and in the development of the soul, that of the irrational preceded that of the rational. None the less, as Aristotle said, the 'care of the [appetitive part] must be for the sake of the reason, and our care of the body for that of the soul.' Hence, the notion of liberal education at this time stressed, in its typically Greek concern for the mean, the need to provide exercises both for the body and the mind — gymnastics and music both played their part. But in so far as the end was rationality fostered by know-ledge, clearly the tendency was to consider knowledge as the more fundamental, for it was the end towards which man strove so as to realise mind, and it produced the knowledge of the Good which was so crucial in the life of the good citizen. My point is that knowledge came to have a particularly important place in the development of the con-cept of liberal education, and that it too was subject to the notion of hierarchy. Plato stressed particularly the roles of arithmetic, geometry, astronomy and music. These had their practical uses, but it was not this aspect of the disciplines that was stressed. Each was regarded as capable of further development beyond its practical uses — there was a hier-archy of relevance, as it were, within each field, so that each could become a vehicle in rising towards 'a comprehension of the essential Form of Goodness'. Arithmetic, for instance, was to be studied 'not like merchants or shopkeepers for purposes of buying and selling, but with a view to war and to help in the conversion of the soul itself from the world of becoming to truth and reality.' These four disciplines were themselves preliminaries to the study of dialectic, which led to the ultimate knowledge. Furthermore, it is made clear that, at least where the preliminary studies of these disciplines are concerned, knowledge of them must be pursued much in the spirit of play, 'because for the free man there should be no element of slavery in learning.' What I have termed the 'tone' or *manner* of the learning is important in Plato as in Aristotle: 'liberality' involves the freedom to take or to leave.

We have now, I hope, distinguished some important elements which characterised the classical expositions of the doctrine of liberal educa-tion. Sustained by a metaphysic of man and a philosophy of the state, in both of which the notion of hierarchy plays a crucial role (so that there are both more important people and more important forms of knowledge, culminating in that knowledge of ultimate reality which is alone the true guide to direct the political activities of the philosopher-king himself), the notion of liberal education comprises both a curriculum and an attitude of mind towards it, what I have termed its social tone or manner. Such a social tone (and, indeed, such a curriculum, in view of what is sought from the various fields of study) is most likely to flourish under a specific set of social conditions, where a particular class in the community, either through birth or merit, has the necessary leisure to pursue its activities in this very specific way, where 'true' knowledge is a form of contemplation rather than a tool; and, in so far as it is a tool, it has been sifted through contemplation before it is brought into play. It must not be forgotten, of course, that the ultimate aim was the creation of the political being. But for Plato (though not for Isocrates or for others of the Sophists, whose attitudes were more pragmatical) action was subordinated to understanding and was only likely to be suffused with right principle when the ultimate reality, the Form of the Good, had been contemplated.

This points to a further dilemma in our understanding of the concept. Was the knowledge gained *ultimately* to be useful or not? Clearly, it was not to be useful in the ordinarily accepted sense: but was it ultimately to issue in action at a higher level – at the highest level, indeed – or was it entirely to be directed to contemplation? Werner Jaeger,[3] in a study 'On the origin and cycle of the philosophical ideal of life' has shown how, in Plato and Aristotle, a tension at certain stages of their careers did exist between the claims of the 'theoretic' and the 'practical' life, so that Plato in his old age tended to resolve the tension between knowledge and action by laying the stress on the former. Clearly, this is a possible development implicit in any idea of knowledge 'for his own sake', as Aristotle puts it, with reference to the individual learner.

In a sense, too, this uncertainty over the possibility of at least a type of use for liberal education – albeit an indirect one – is not unrelated to the dilemma to which I referred at the beginning, the uncertainty as to whether it is the approach, the 'tone' which matters, or the exact nature of the knowledge assimilated, to one's understanding of liberal knowledge: whether it is the manner or the matter that is crucial. For clearly the leisured approach could lead to knowledge that is purely contemplative, its aim being to relate man to the universe, to 'explain' the human predicament. And if the knowledge becomes purely a matter of science, in the old sense of the word, this can easily be divorced from ethics, which would imply preparation for action.

II

These dilemmas are illustrated in the further history of the notion. In the development of Rome – much influenced as it was by Greek ideas – the liberal arts were initially intended to supply means for the production of orators, and thus maintained a close connection with political life. Indeed, it was the pragmatical Isocrates who influenced Roman practice, with his stress on the direct implications of eloquence, rather than Plato. The need for leisure is still stressed, however: 'He does not seem to me a free man who does not sometimes do nothing,' wrote Cicero. But with the rise of autocratic government and the death of the Republic, learning came to be divorced from political action: 'we learn for school, not life,' complained Seneca. The learning came to serve the needs of private virtue rather than of public involvement.

The early Christians reacted strongly against pagan learning: 'the same mouth cannot sing the praises of Jupiter and the praises of Christ,' wrote Gregory the Great, on hearing that the Bishop of Vienne was lecturing on pagan authors. But inevitably, a way to compromise was found. St Augustine of Hippo accepted the disciplines of classical liberal studies (the seven liberal arts of grammar, rhetoric and dialectic (the trivium), and music, geometry, arithmetic and astronomy (the quadrivium), are first explicitly mentioned in the first century before Christ) and sought their exemplifications in Christian writers; he also provided text-books containing readings in each of the arts. Cassiodorus, more than a century later, also describes the seven arts in a book intended for the monks of his foundation. Significantly, he derives the notion of 'liberal' not from 'free man', but from the Latin word for book. Clearly, in a religion based on a book, 'the new faith was logically committed to the fostering of some knowledge of letters.'[4] Furthermore, during the medieval period knowledge was based on authority, rather than observation. Hence, education was bookish and academic rather than for use, for, as Professor Charlton[5] has pointed out,

> It was no longer the free man, nor the lay gentleman, but the cleric for whom such an education was deemed appropriate, and it was in the monasteries and later in the cathedral schools that such education was to be found.

The general aim of such arts (of which the trivium was the more widely studied and grammar the only art universally fostered; they were later taught in the universities, as preparation for the study of theology, law and medicine), was not primarily for the exercise of politics but for the pursuit of that combination of philosophy and theology known as scholasticism. The physical side of the traditional Greek liberal education degenerated into the hard physical labour of the monastic life;

sports were kept alive in the physical recreations of the feudal nobility.

Thus, a liberal education, having dropped its connection with the *polis*, had no longer any specific relation with action per se. Salvation was the aim of the Middle Ages, its means the *vita contemplativa*, the *vita solitaria*. Knowledge retained its metaphysical support – but with emphasis on matter rather than on manner. Soon, however, medieval stress on otherworldliness was to give way before a revived humanist emphasis on civic busyness and virtue; the rediscovery and reappraisal indicated an alternative route to salvation through the practice of the civic virtues. Practical knowledge derived from the ancients rather than speculation is sought after and an emphasis on ethics replaces the medieval concern with metaphysics and natural philosophy. In the revived interest in classical literature, the humanists of the Renaissance discovered a pattern of human existence which enabled them, once more, to participate in the life of the *polis*. Man's freedom of choice comes to the centre of the picture and is reflected in the increased concern for education: 'I study much that I may be an educated man, but more that I may be good and free. The one makes one feel right, and the other makes one live rightly,'[6] wrote Vergerio. Erasmus and More both stressed that it was the practical, political wisdom of the classical writers that was of value.

Again, both matter and manner – one could indeed add manners – are important; for the new humanist training was as much concerned with elegance and style – 'eloquence' – as with content in pursuit of its persuasive purpose, and physical grace was inculcated as well as mental power. Theorists had in mind an aristocracy, those who could support themselves in leisure, essential for the mastery of the ancient authors; for leisure should be adorned by letters, and made gracious by courtesy. There was a return to the Greek concern for the body as well as the mind; physical culture contributed once more to the education of the whole man, sometimes as a preparation for war (hence medieval rather than classical in origin), though often for purposes of pleasing in one's relationship with others. Play and pleasure were concomitants of the new humanistic education, harsh discipline to be avoided: 'Teaching by beating', Erasmus pointed out, 'is not a liberal education' – naturally enough, when the aim was *sprezzatura*, effortlessness. As for matter, the humanists struck at the prevailing Aristotelianism, which had led to scholastic hair-splitting, and turned to the classical interest in man: 'In the literatures of Greece and Rome,' Erasmus surmised, is 'all the knowledge we recognise as vital to mankind.'[7] Christianity was not necessarily abandoned, of course; it was merely 'humanised'.

Thus what occurs is a fusion of the old knightly concern for the physical life with a new emphasis on the need for a lettered and poised aristocracy: as Woodward[8] expresses it a reconciliation of the old type with the new — the knightly with the civic and the scholarly — produced an ideal of personality, of the complete man of modern society, which stands for the final and harmonious picture of personality as the Renaissance had fashioned it.

What was aimed at was the well-rounded man, later to merge into the 'compleat gentleman'. In his highest manifestation, the sense of duty and obligation implicit in Elyot's governor was combined with the *urbanitas* and *galanterie* of Castiglione's courtier. Both exercised their skills in forms of ruling.

Again, then, we have a liberal education which is poised between matter and manner. The ideal of civic virtue upheld is modelled on ideas derived from Cicero and Quintilian, looking back ultimately to Isocrates, rather than on Plato's philosopher-king, and his search for the Form of the Good. It was, that is to say, more immediately and directly practical than Plato might have liked. It was therefore social and literary rather than metaphysical in character, but it was certainly not directly vocational, in the sense that it was concerned with earning a living, or involved participation in illiberal occupations.[9] It differed from the Greek, however, in that it involved an ideal drawn from an older and past civilisation, rather than one directly drawn from the culture with which it was concerned. The Greek ideal arose out of specific contemporary conditions and the efforts of theorists to cope with them; the Renaissance conception involved the imposition of an historical pattern at the moment when the culture which sustained it contained within itself the seeds of a profound change.[10]

Yet the new urbanity and political practicality of the Renaissance led ultimately to the development of science, technology and industrialisation; it marked a decisive stage in the change-over from one order of reality to another, from the reality of the unworldly unseen, the intangible, to the order of sensory experience which modern science accepts as the only reality. As a stage in that development was the change-over of an educational ideal based ultimately on a purely metaphysical foundation to one based on an historical foundation. The ultimate liberality of Plato depended on the Form of the Good; the ultimate liberality of the Renaissance depended on an historical, essentially political literature. In both the case of the Greek and the humanist, the ultimate controlling factor was a specific social and political need: and in both cases, the notion of aristocracy, with its peculiar social tone, was at the centre of the picture.

III

In the production of Greek citizen, Roman orator and Renaissance all-round man, then, matter and manner are held together in a subtle tension; both enter as equally relevant in the definition of the appropriate type. In the further development of the particular idea of the *classical* liberal education, which has lasted until nearly our own times, matter gradually overwhelmed, in real importance, manner.

In its later days, an education in the classics was supported by the doctrine of formal discipline, with its emphasis on the production of the rational man; mind and its training now comes to predominate in a way which is symptomatic of the whole development of education. The spread of faculty psychology supported the need to train the various aspects of men's minds. Even if the content of studies is forgotten, it was thought, there is still the advantage of having given the mind a training which it could then transfer to the more mundane matters of daily life – this is what might be termed the 'mental gymnastics' view of education. Mathematics, too, was much approved for this purpose, following Locke who considered mathematics important 'to make anyone reason well'. The difficulty of mathematics and the classics was an added attraction – they constituted a sort of *rite de passage* by which the mind of the growing boy was inured to hardship and trained to endure. Elegant and gracious behaviour no longer received equal attention. The classics were valued for their purely mental qualities, and degenerated into a narrower, more purely linguistic study.

Latterly, other subjects were advanced on the grounds that they, too, provided the necessary disciplinary content. But the doctrine of transfer of training, which had sustained that of formal discipline, became highly suspect; the notion of the specificity of disciplines was substituted. A disciple of Herbart wrote that there are 'as many kinds of formal education as there are essentially different spheres of intellectual employment.'

For the time when the traditional view of the classics contracted to an increased emphasis on their formal qualities, their usefulness in the training of mind, coincided with a period when new disciplines fought for attention, disciplines which had come to significance in the immediate post-Renaissance period of the seventeenth century; and what these disciplines most emphasised was the role of cognition, the functioning of mind. Greek and Roman orator, and Renaissance universal man had emphasised the importance of 'knowledge' in the doctrine of *doctus orator*; but it was a knowledge suffused with moral insight and deployed, as has been insisted on, with a persuasiveness of manner which accorded 'manners' equal weight with content. But manners (and indeed, morality) were irrelevant to the new kind of knowledge which was derived from the direct contact of mind and world. The challenge of scientific observation led to a profound philosophical search for the true bases of our knowledge or 'understanding'. As a result, attention was focused on mind to an unprecedented extent, and on the knowledge of which the mind was constituted. As Professor Gellner has put it, before Descartes knowing was a process in the world, one of the many aspects of living; after Descartes, the world became an event within knowledge.

The new knowledge, too, is a much more 'democratic' knowledge — at least initially and in principle. It is derived from a common observation of a common world, not from an arcane literature. This was a knowledge which arose out of the practical immediacies of life, the desire to control and manipulate nature (as Bacon indicated, this new knowledge was 'power'); it implied a new set of social demands, was indicative of the rise of a new class in the state, the bourgeoisie, who had long urged the importance of a new, more practically oriented education to underpin their commercial, mercantile and even industrial enterprises. The new concern is with busyness, not leisure; the new knowledge was open, and not esoteric, the prerogative of an elite, as the classics had always been; it depended exclusively on the functioning of the understanding in its contacts with the external world, not on subtleties of social tone or the nuances of language.

Yet, of course, the idea of liberal education survives but in terms which concentrate exclusively on matter. It has sought an institutional basis in the schools and universities, despite the fact that the logic of events — especially the need for specialisation — has tended to pull both in a rather different direction. Matthew Arnold, following the example of Von Humboldt in making a synthesis between the humanism of the old world and the understanding, scientific and mathematical, of the new, based his recommendations for liberal education on the idea of the circle of knowledge, comprising the study of the humanities and that of the world. He believed that those with aptitudes for the study of nature should have some notion of the humanities; while those with aptitudes for the humanities should have some notion of the phenomena and laws of nature. This, indeed, was the general revised view of a liberal education in the nineteenth century. It concentrated on the expansion of mind through knowledge. Herbart considered that '*realia* are at least as much a legitimate part of a complete education' as humanistic elements, and stressed the need for a 'many-sided interest'. Arnold's view that 'The secondary school has essentially for its object a general liberal culture' was institutionally enshrined in the Regulations of 1904, with their concern for a 'sound general education'. This has been the impetus behind the grammar school, however little its inhabitants may have accepted its full implications. In the nineteenth-century university, Newman remains the great exponent of that intellectual training proper to such a milieu:[11]

> This process of training, by which the intellect, instead of being formed or sacrificed to some particular or accidental purpose, some specific trade or profession, or study or science, is disciplined for its own sake, for the perception of its own proper object, and for its own highest culture, is called Liberal Education.

This is simply one of a long line of similar formulations in the changed social and intellectual circumstances of a technical age which I briefly alluded to earlier. After the comparative narrowness of the stress on the disciplinary value of mathematics and the classics, what is interesting about these formulations is the attempt, once more, to stress the *range* of understanding necessary for liberal education; whatever else liberal education is conceived as becoming in the changed social circumstances, it is regarded as being resolutely *not* specialist. As with Aristotle, too great concentration on any one aspect is regarded as inherently narrowing and therefore not liberating. At the same time, there is no mistaking the fact that a new intensity characterises the emphasis on the 'circle of knowledge' which was lacking in the older view of a liberal education.

Indeed, the most interesting feature of the effort to cope with the new situation has been the attempt to assimilate what, quite specifically, the ancient world resolutely excluded from its concept of liberal education — the technical. Traditionally the technical was always regarded as too narrowly vocational to qualify. Here at least the situation has changed. As a result of the immense development of the pure and applied sciences during the last 100 years, technical understanding has gained immensely in what Professor Peters has termed 'cognitive perspective'. The technical, indeed, has turned into the technological, with the vast extension of theoretical understanding which that change implies.

The best attempt to exploit the intellectual potentialities of modern technical knowledge as a means to liberal education is, of course, that of A.N. Whitehead, in his essay on 'Technical education and its relation to science and literature'.[12] The argument sets out to resolve the conflict between the rival attractions of action and contemplation as the final fruits of a liberal education. I have drawn attention to the fact that throughout its history the purpose of liberal education was usually (not always) a particular type of highly sophisticated activity only, arising out of subject-matter studied at leisure, without immediate practical interest. Only when he had acquired wisdom was the product of liberal education fitted for that highest of all functions, the direction of the body politic: this was the action permitted by the idealism of Plato as it was by the classicism of Jowett, the latter of whom saw in the liberality of ancient literature a propaedeutic to the rule of empire. Whitehead's attempt is to carry the ultimate practicality of liberal education into many more spheres, as befits a democratic age when it is assumed that every man is his own philosopher-king:

> Action and our implication in the transition of events amid the inevitable bond of cause to effect are fundamental. An education which strives to divorce intellectual or aesthetic life from these fundamental facts carries with it the decadence of civilisation. Essentially culture should be for action . . . .

Whitehead's conclusion is that[13]

> The antithesis between a technical and a liberal education is fallacious. There can be no adequate technical education which is not liberal, and no liberal education which is not technical: that is, no education which does not impart both technique and intellectual vision.

There are, however, several points to be made. Whitehead continues by widening the scope of liberal knowledge to comprise the circle of knowledge – involving 'the literary curriculum, the scientific curriculum, the technical curriculum'; and he purports to discover elements of each in each. But this, of course, involves to some extent an abuse of terms. He speaks, for instance, of the role of technique in the study of language; but this shifts the meaning of the word 'technical'. When we speak of the technique of writing, we merely refer to the way in which we go about setting our thoughts down on paper; and that involves quite different elements of judgment from what are involved in the techniques of the technical properly so called. (The same mistake is involved in the more frequent misuse of the injunction to teach children to think, as if there were a global activity called thinking, as opposed to particular operations of thought – thinking historically, thinking scientifically, etc., involving different modes of mental operation in each case.) When Whitehead considers, then, that there is no liberal education that is not technical, I cannot help thinking that this involves a shift in the use of the word 'technical' from the way in which it is used in the first part of the proposition.

His analysis of 'technical' education as such is also open to some questioning. He finds that both scientific and aesthetic elements are involved. The scientific element we may readily admit, especially in the more complex technical processes; the aesthetic, as an essential element in the technical, is a more dubious starter. The aim of a technical development is efficiency; if in the process something aesthetically pleasing is produced, this is a by-product rather than something essential to the undertaking. To make a cup is to make something capable of holding water; it need not be a beautiful cup. And indeed, it is only when sensibilities other than those developed by the technical as such are brought into play that men come to demand something pleasing as well as something which fulfils its function. Where the technical is being used with reference to machine industry, for instance, Veblen's analysis seems the truer:[14]

> What the discipline of the machine industry inculcates . . . is regularity of sequence and mechanical precision; and the intellectual outcome is an habitual resort to terms of measurable cause and effect, together with a relative disparagement of such exercise of the intellectual faculties as does not run on these lines. . . . The resultant discipline is a discipline in the handling of impersonal facts for mechanical effect.

Whitehead's essay, it seems to me, is full of such fallacies and half truths; yet is has clearly exercised a considerable influence on modern thinking about liberal education – for example, in the Spens Report. Nevertheless, when all criticisms have been made it is true that Whitehead ultimately does not base his view of liberal education on the supposed virtues of the technical but on the idea of the circle of knowledge; and it is here that attempts to define modern liberal education in general fall into agreement. It could almost be said that such attempts are defined in terms of what they are reacting against: the need imposed by our civilisation to produce the specialised expert. It is this which marks the varied attempts of theorists like Professor Phenix in America and Professor Hirst in this country: the attempt to work out different areas of meaning, knowledge and understanding, all of which play their part in the formation of the liberally educated person. Professor Hirst, in his essay on 'Liberal Education', reasserts what was basically the Greek conception without its metaphysical overtones: 'It is an education concerned directly with the development of the mind in rational knowledge, whatever form that freely takes.'[15] The same attempts at intellectual breadth mark the framing of curricula – Harvard's general education and the comprehensive school's common core, which is the grammar school's offering diluted with varying degrees of water in desperation at the lack of response it invokes at certain levels.

Yet in all these attempts to redefine liberal education in the changed circumstances of the nineteenth and twentieth centuries one crucial feature of traditional liberal education has been forgotten – the element of *sprezzatura*, of play, of what I have referred to as social tone, of manner. To this extent modern liberal education has succumbed to the enemy it is supposed to combat, the peculiar intensity which marks all expertise, all concentration on a narrow field.

This element of *sprezzatura* is terribly difficult to define in the changed circumstances of the modern world, in the traditions of which work has taken on a new intensity (divided specifically from leisure as never in the past) and play has degenerated into entertainment and distraction. I would hate to seem to give any sanction to an irresponsible dilettantism based on a pretentious egocentrism; such was not indeed implied by Greek notions of *arete*. Perhaps the nearest I can get to what I think is implied is to be found in T.S. Eliot's injunction 'Teach us to care and not to care,' or in D.H. Lawrence's conception of insouciance: 'They care! They simply are eaten up with caring,' he wrote of the middle classes; 'There simply is a deadly breach between actual living and this abstract caring.' Nietzsche, too, grasps something of the situation in his criticisms of the man of theory, and of the false optimism which the worship of knowledge has engendered. All three, in very different ways, have stressed the need for more attention to the 'instinctual' life – of which, traditionally, what was implicit in 'manner' formed a part.

For, as I understand it, *sprezzatura* protests against both the mode and the manner of modern understanding. It protests against both the excessive faith in knowledge and understanding as the modern world seeks these, and against the intensity of the search after them. The solution is not an abandonment of what knowledge has brought with it but a balancing with other modes, so that both the strengths and the limitations of 'understanding' become apparent. And this is a way which is proper to an essentially limited creature like man in whom a calm assessment of his own limitations would seem to be the beginning of wisdom. Perhaps, too, this would promote a greater sense of balance; and surely this sense of balance was one of the first virtues that a liberal education, in the dawn of its history, set out to promote. And perhaps today, too, in our pragmatic age, with its crude emphasis on immediate utility, we need, more than ever, the sense of enlargement and freedom from immediate decision-making which a liberal education, infused with an element of 'play', would afford; and there is a sense in which ultimately and paradoxically this is the most useful form of education we can have. For, traditionally, the notion of a liberal education was at once wider – in that it encompassed more aspects of the personality – if in certain respects less intense; and yet, for much of its history, it preserved a strong sense of social responsibility.

Chapter 5

The arts in education

I

One of the best approaches to a contemporary consideration of the role of the arts in education is to see the whole problem in its historical context and evolution. There was a time when certain of the arts were very central to the whole educational system: and perhaps if we go back to that period we will be able to illumine certain of our contemporary dilemmas and difficulties.

II

The word 'arts' is itself somewhat ambiguous. It can refer to the artefacts, which are the products of artistic endeavour — especially, of course, to painting with which the word 'art' is very often associated. It can also be used to refer to the theory of practice explicitly articulated of some highly developed complex skill. For instance one refers to the arts and implies a body of achievements, a collection of artefacts, paintings, sculptings, musical scores, poems, novels and the like; and one also refers to the 'art' of poetry, of painting, or sculpting, and of other highly developed human activities like politics, for instance ('the art of politics') when one is using it in the theoretical sense. Indeed, I propose historically to go back to the period when the theoretical elucidation of the arts was first articulated (in post-classical Western Europe), the period of the Renaissance. It was during the Renaissance that the literary arts, at least in humanist theory, were at the very centre of educational concern. For the Renaissance was a period when artefacts were produced in very large numbers, but also when important steps were taken in theorising about the nature of these artefacts. We can therefore not only point to the centrality of the literary arts in Renaissance education but we can also discover why they were thought to be important. Let me then first say a few words briefly about the literary arts which occupied this central position in humanist Renaissance education: what they were and why they were regarded as important. Then we can look at how gradually others of the arts came to seem of almost equal importance – painting, sculpting and so on.

III

In the medieval period, at school level people studied what was called the trivium, which consisted of three disciplines – grammar, logic and rhetoric. The emphasis in the medieval period was on grammar (which of course was Latin, not English, grammar), and on logic, which constituted an essential element in theological philosophical argument; the orientation of the Middle Ages towards the theological necessitated a strong stress on the science of argument. But that changed with the Renaissance. What now came to be emphasised was rhetoric, for social and political reasons, for purposes of persuasion. The new educational emphasis arose originally in Italy, where the development of the Italian city state created a need for an educated bureaucracy. This bureaucracy was to be educated in a classical tongue and particularly in that aspect of the classical tongue which came under the heading of rhetoric, derived, of course, from the classical notion of the orator.

The orator played an important political role because, as we were still in an oral age, political action could be influenced by the power of persuasive speech. So the first thing to be said about the literary arts in the Renaissance is that they were directed towards very specific social and political tasks. In a developing society, made up in Italy of small principalities but, north of the Alps, of national societies which were gradually evolving out of the feudal societies of the Middle Ages, the humanist training in rhetoric in the literary arts came to play an important, central role. These societies needed lawyers and behind the legal training there was necessarily a rhetorical training in the arts of speech. They needed ambassadors and ambassadorial functions had to be fulfilled with elegance and a certain power of eloquence. They needed men able to persuade popular assemblies of citizens in the more 'democratic' societies, or rulers in those under the guidance of prince or king. And so this training had an important central moral and political role in the life of these societies. The literary arts were accepted as providing just such a training. Stylistically they afforded models in the work of the great classical writers like Cicero. (Latin had never died, but medieval Latin had never paid the attention to stylistic purity and eloquence which the humanist did.) Secondly, in the experience of the classical past, there was thought to be important moral guidance for the elucidation of contemporary problems. The classical experience was something which arose out of an essentially political literature, for Roman and Greek writings to a very considerable extent are oriented towards politics, a politics which was sustained by the moral philosophies of the ancients, and thus, in the range of its moral possibilities should not be confused with the politicisation of the modern totalitarian state. What indeed tended to happen in the Renaissance period was the gradual replacement of the Christian moral emphasis by a more humanistic classical emphasis derived from their literature. (That is a statement that needs to be regarded with some care because the humanists still remained primarily Christian; but by and large the classical experience now began to be absorbed and play a central role in the social and political life of the countries influenced by the humanistic revolution.)

Gradually, too, the other arts — painting, sculpting, architecture — began to play an increasing cultural and social role. There was a time when such arts had been regarded as servile. The medieval painter was primarily a craftsman: the Renaissance painter, because he gradually began to theorise, and thus to lift the whole intellectual level of the work that he was doing, improved his status, until by the time we reach the high Renaissance people like Leonardo da Vinci and Michelangelo were wooed by the monarchs of Europe. (Was it not true that the Emperor Charles V himself actually bent down and picked up the paintbrush of the great artist Titian when he dropped it? What more splendid indication of the status assigned to a great artist could there be than that the Emperor himself should bend down and pick up the paintbrush of a common painter!) So, during this period artists come to improve their status enormously. From being simple craftsmen they became centrally employed in the whole business of government — as agents, one might almost say, of state prestige and propaganda. Kings and princes quarrelled, for prestige reasons, in order to get their attention. They were regarded as a means by which the state achieved fame and acclaim. So we have now a society where the arts occupied a very important and crucial role. I said earlier a 'central' role; perhaps it's just as well to remember that the scholastic philosophy still continued and therefore there were those who regarded the arts with a somewhat equivocal eye for reasons that I will reveal shortly. In general, however, they now occupied a crucially important role. And indeed if one looks at the educational theory of the Renaissance one will see that at its high-water mark it recommends making a human being as if he were himself a work of art. This is the central notion of that great book of Renaissance education, Castiglione's book *The Courtier*. The concepts which were applied to the education of the courtier are concepts which are really derived from the arts. Particularly central (this is a very important notion) is the concept of imitation. (It is important to remember that when one is talking about courtiers, one is talking about the great officers of state, people who occupied a central political role. The Cecils in this country – Queen Elizabeth's courtiers – were people who were the equivalent of prime ministers and cabinet ministers today. As they occupied that sort of role, their education was a matter of the gravest importance.) How then did one form a courtier? The central notion involved was that of imitation, as I have indicated, a word which is crucial in the whole aesthetic of the Renaissance. Imitation in what way? Castiglione indicates that the ideal courtier must learn by watching other courtiers, choose the best aspects of the behaviour of several, the best features possible to help form his own behaviour. Now this constitutes the essence of the Renaissance aesthetic; it turned to the past, to the classical experience, as I have already indicated. It chose its models from the most elegantly stylistic of the classical writers, writers like Cicero, who were regarded as the most eloquent.

There was, however, another aspect to imitation, and it is very important for the development of my argument that I make this clear. Although imitation involved very much an absorption, of a sort that nowadays we can hardly conceive, of the classical experience through its literature, at its best the Renaissance concept of imitation did not mean mere *copying*. It meant the absorption of the experience for its redeployment with a certain measure of autonomy and freedom. It meant that what the child did when he went to school, what the young apprentice did when he went into the workshop of the artist, was to learn his craft by the most careful absorption of past models. Then, if he had any real genius, he didn't become what was sneeringly referred to as an 'ape of Cicero' (i.e. a mere copyist), but was able to redeploy this tremendously detailed and careful training, with an element of what the Italians called *sprezzatura*; and this concept of *sprezzatura* is essential for the full understanding of the doctrine of imitation, both with reference to the aesthetic education of the Renaissance period and the education of the courtier. *Sprezzatura* means 'effortlessness', about the best translation one can get. It implied an internalisation of previous models so detailed and precise as greatly to facilitate expression and give it an appearance of effortless ease.

I have drawn attention to the fuller implications of the notion of 'imitation' in my chapter on 'The parochialism of the present'. It produced, as I have pointed out, the miracle of Shakespeare who 'never originated anything, literary types, verse forms, plots, etc. etc. and yet he is one of the most original authors who has ever lived.' We know that Shakespeare stole his plots, his characters, his words, scenes, and yet he is the most complete example of this essence of Renaissance education, this ability to absorb and redeploy in a way which makes him the greatest, most complete, and most original of writers. This paradox of an imitation that produced a profound originality is central to my theme.

IV

The ultimate purpose of all this education was undoubtedly moral. The idea of the courtier was that he should learn the arts of persuasion in order to give good moral advice to his prince or king. This was the function of this essentially literary education, one which should provide a moral insight into the contemporary problems on which the courtier, the equivalent, as I have indicated, of a modern minister, had to advise his prince.

So behind Renaissance theorising and practice were notions of truth and moral purpose. In architecture, for instance, buildings were based on notions of mathematical proportions which were supposed to reflect the fundamental harmonies of the universe. So the Renaissance accepted the notion of 'forming' or 'moulding' the child to a preordained, a pre-established pattern. As Erasmus put it, 'Homines non nascuntur sed finguntur' (men are not born but made, fashioned). That is why the disciplines of Renaissance education were so severe — they looked back to former models which were laid down for their guidance in the literature of the classics.

But in its literary form, despite their acceptance of the classical experience, there was a question that nagged at them as indeed it had nagged at some of the ancients (including Plato). Most of the literature was overtly and intentionally fictional; and someone was bound sooner or later to raise the question 'How can the fictional be real?' How can what is admittedly a fiction reveal the forms of reality, of moral truth, for instance? If one paints a picture or writes a story, however it is intended to copy or represent the real, there is a sense in which it isn't real. So though the Renaissance artist did claim to be dealing with moral reality, he was doing it through various literary or artistic devices and these devices would seem to be false to some people because they were fictional. Shakespeare placed a number of his plays in historical circumstances but the history was often not very good history. The Roman historians themselves were notoriously inaccurate in their historical accounts, as Renaissance historians discovered when they investigated. So this was a fatal flaw, this question as to how what was essentially something artificial, something fabricated, could be regarded as indicative of reality. It raised the whole question of the relationship between the artist and nature, for instance; how one interpreted the concept of the 'natural'. Renaissance writers and painters solved the problem to some extent by saying that it was natural for human beings to be artificial – that they didn't just *live* their lives but through their consciousness in a sense *made* them.

Yet obviously there were senses in which the 'artificial' couldn't be the 'natural', true to nature. It depended on one's usage of that very difficult and very complex term, the 'natural'. Clearly, there are senses of 'natural' which would seem the total opposite to the artificial – the two things are often thought to be in direct conflict. The 'natural' then is equated with that which hasn't been made, interfered with by man – the 'real' in *this* sense.[1]

Then the very art of rhetoric itself, the very notion of persuasion opens itself to all sorts of abuses. It's all very well saying that rhetoric is for the purposes of truth and virtue but evil men could very easily use persuasive language for their own ends. The person who explored this problem is Shakespeare, as I have indicated. 'So may the outward shows be least themselves: The world is still deceived with ornament,' says Bassanio in *The Merchant of Venice*. And there is the pervasiveness of disguise all through the Shakespearean corpus; disguise plays a crucial and important role – and disguise implies deceit.

Historically what happened was that early scientists began to explore a different conception of reality; so what came to seem to be real in behaviour was no longer this Renaissance artistic experience, but regularities noted as a result of applying quantitative mathematical techniques to observed phenomena – in other words, science. Francis Bacon wrote at the very same time as Shakespeare, and Bacon, who was the great propagandist of science, pointed out that poetry was 'feigned history' which submitted 'the shows of things to the desires of the mind whereas reason doth buckle and bow the mind unto the nature of things.' What he is in effect defining is a new difference between fact and fiction: poetry he dismisses as fictional – the realities are to be found in reason and the nature of things. And the nature of things now was revealed in their regularities, which of course provide the basis of the scientific outlook. Locke, whose thoughts on education were of the profoundest interest in the eighteenth century, went so far as to suggest that if a child had a poetic vein parents should labour to have it stifled as much as possible, for poetry was untrue to life and unprofitable into the bargain – as he put it, it is very seldom that anyone discovers mines of gold or silver on Parnassus. In any case, mixing with artists took one into bad company and thus was no place for a gentleman. (Although I said that great artists like Michelangelo and Leonardo achieved tremendous social prestige, the ordinary average actor, painter, dancer, playwright retained a pretty lowly sort of status and did indeed down to Victorian times.)

So, we begin now to detect a very equivocal attitude towards the arts. In the eighteenth century they were no longer regarded as central to the life of the society but took on much more the function of orna- ment. No longer did they afford an insight into reality. Instead, they provided a source of pleasure. In their country houses gentlemen collected artefacts indicative of their elegance and taste, as a matter largely of prestige; they served for delight but did not inform the real business of living. This was increasingly administered to by develop- ments of a technical and scientific nature. One can begin to detect the change in Rousseau's analysis of one of Aesop's fables, 'The Fox and the Crow'. This provides a perfect example of what could happen to the poetic. The story is of the fox and the crow and the cheese and how the fox got the cheese from the crow, who was holding it in his beak, by means of flattery. He thus persuaded the crow to open his beak, the cheese fell out and the fox got it. Now Rousseau analyses this little fable (which is the sort of thing which children love) and he asked literal questions of fact about it: for example, how could the fox smell the cheese if the crow was right up in the tree? These are not the sort of questions intended in the fable. Implicit in them is a quite different view of reality, a view of reality which doesn't raise questions for children and wouldn't worry most readers of Aesop's fables; but Rousseau was judging the poetic licence of the fable and suggesting that acceptance of it implied that one was fostering in children a love of falsehood. Another progressive educationist, Maria Montessori, another 100 years further on, banished fairy-tales altogether on the grounds that they weren't true, or scientifically accurate, for this now provided the criterion of reality.

There was a reaction against this depreciation of the poetic fictional, of course. Towards the end of the eighteenth century the Romantics once more stressed the centrality of the arts, arguing that they formed a crucial part of human experience. But of course they now existed in a socially much more precarious way than during the period of the humanists. What was now emphasised was *individual* experience which hadn't received the same stress in Renaissance humanism. Humanists had regarded the arts as essentially social. The Romantics were more antagonistic to their society; they often convey a sense of being against the dominating trends and place a stress on individual experience which can very easily become eccentricity and indeed lapse into solipsism. Secondly, they tended to over-emphasise the importance of feeling. Because science depended on rationality the Romantics as a counter- blast stressed feeling: 'Oh for a life of sensations rather than thoughts,' Keats had said. This emphasis on feeling, as something over against the cognitive, induced a split in consciousness which the Renaissance, I don't think, to that extent shared. In the Renaissance there existed, at its best, an extraordinary balance of both cognition and feeling: this is certainly highly characteristic of Shakespeare and Donne.

In the Romantic period, then, there is first this concern increasingly with individual over against social experience, and, second, a broad emphasis on feeling and the primitive as opposed to the more sophisticated and the cognitive. As a result, something obviously happens to the moral aspect. The artist in his antagonistic attitude to the society can tend also to become something of an immoralist. (This was the situation which Henry James depicted in his novel *Roderick Hudson*, where James examines the position of the artist and concludes against his immoralism. Roderick Hudson himself, a young artist, is condemned because he doesn't accept the normal moral conventions of society.)

Now we must remember that it is within the ambience of the Romantic revolt that we today find our current educational dilemmas. They are particularly to be noted in the extremities of romanticism which I will term 'avant-gardism'. This has become manifest in the twentieth century in a very wide variety of different movements of an artistic and literary type. Just think of the 'isms' there are in art: Surrealism (I am not putting them in any order), Expressionism, Constructivism, Futurism, as well as op art, pop art — one could list many more. From the end of the nineteenth century there has been a continual series of movements manifesting themselves on an individualistic or small-group basis, in many cases becoming more and more extreme in their extravagant claims or in their antagonism to the bourgeois world, the world of ordinary everyday life. (Mario Praz has analysed something of this sense of antagonism which has been implicit in the Romantic movement from the beginning in his book *The Romantic Agony*.) The Romantics have found ordinary life over-rationalistic, unwilling to give feeling its due place. The breakdown of J.S. Mill in the face of his father's excessively intellectual educational regimen lends some credence to their claims.

Now this split between the artist and ordinary society has had grave effects, artistically, as Picasso, one of the supremely great artists of the twentieth century, realised. In some respects, Picasso was the spoilt child of the twentieth century; on the one hand the twentieth century has spoilt its artists and on the other hand it has treated them with contempt. Picasso died a millionaire many times over; yet, unhappily he never really received the criticism that he should have done and therefore he degenerated too often into sheer foolishness. (The supremely foolish twentieth-century manifestation was Dadaism, a childish reaction to the First World War.) Picasso made an extremely interesting comment about the disintegration of the whole of the artistic tradition of his own times, which forms one of the very crucial and fundamental problems which the arts in education currently face:

As soon as art had lost all link with tradition, and the kind of liberation that came in with Impressionism permitted every painter to do what he wanted to do, painting was finished. When they decided it was the painters' sensations and emotions that mattered, (that is to say in expressionism) and every man could recreate painting as he understood it from any basis whatever, then there was no more painting; there were only individuals

That's what I have just said about the individualistic aspect.[2]

Sculpture died the same death. Beginning with Van Gogh, however great we may be, we are all, in a measure autodidacts, you might almost say primitive painters. Painters no longer live within a tradition so each of us must recreate an entire language. Every painter of our times is fully authorised to recreate that language from A to Z. No criterion can be applied to him a priori since we don't believe in rigid standards any longer. In a sense there is a liberation but at the same time it is an enormous limitation.

One remembers the story about Renoir told by his son in *Renoir My Father* by Jean Renoir, the cinema director. On one occasion Renoir was sitting with some friends in a café; they were talking about medieval painters – and one of them pointed out that they did nothing else but paint pictures of Madonnas and children. 'Ah,' said Renoir, leaning back, 'what freedom'. Once the implications of that anecdote have been grasped, the whole of the modern dilemma is revealed. As Picasso pointed out, modern freedom was at once[3]

a liberation and at the same time an enormous limitation because when the individuality of the artist begins to express itself what the artist gains in the way of liberty he loses in the way of order, and when you are no longer able to attach yourself to an order basically that's very bad.

It was just such an order that the medieval and Renaissance painter, for all his restriction of subject-matter, belonged to; and Renoir saw that such an order constituted liberty in quite a different sense from that prevailing today.

V

Now let us turn to education. This much time has been spent analysing previous artistic movements because it is within the spiritual ambience created by romantic avant-gardism and expressionism that romantic progressivism, it seems to me, became the temporary educational orthodoxy, at least among educationists. (Perhaps it had rather less impact in schools than it did among educational theorists, but it has still had a potent influence on practice during the last thirty years.) So I look upon the progressive movement as it manifested itself especially after the Second World War as coming within the spiritual ambience of the Romantic movement. This romantic progressivism, manifested in child centredness and a concern for lifting restraints and allowing self-expression, was at least an attempt to reinstate the centrality of the arts as forms of impulse release. One remembers that famous statement of Rousseau: 'The first impulses of nature are always right.' Personal artistic expressiveness was supposed to have a quasi-therapeutic value in our over-rationalistic civilisation. Herbert Read, the great modern exponent of education in the arts considered that: 'The secret of our collective ills is to be traced to the suppression of spontaneous creative ability of the individual.' Yet, in the light of this historical analysis, one needs to seize upon that word 'spontaneous' and ask what it implies. Is it *sprezzatura*, the 'spontaneity' that comes from the deep absorption of previous experience or is it simply primitive impulse release? Behind the dilemma lurks one of the fundamental issues for educationists of our time.

The central concepts of romantic progressivism have been self-expression, creativity, spontaneity, and of course nature and its derivatives, 'natural', etc. 'Nature' as I have indicated is a word that should be treated with the greatest restraint and care. It's perhaps the most ambiguous word in the English language. (I believe that a history of the word 'nature' would encompass much if not most of Western thought. Arthur Lovejoy, for instance, distinguished sixty meanings in the eighteenth century.) It's a word that when one uses it one should always stop and think. What is 'natural'? Where humans are concerned, it so often implies simply an alternative form of artifice from that currently pervasive. But of course it has a basic content – I mean it's 'natural' that human beings have two eyes, a nose, a mouth, and they live by breathing: these are 'natural' basic elements, they're inescapable. It's when one gets beyond this purely physical sense, to the more sophisticated uses of the word that it becomes such an ambiguous concept. Very often, of course, it's used as an emotive approval word as a means of beating down antagonism. One says: 'It is only natural that he should do that' – sometimes as a means of excusing some quite gross piece of behaviour. This raises the issue as to what is the relationship between what is natural and what is civilised. Is it not perhaps natural for human beings to be civilised? And does this imply not simply impulse release but some degree of restraint, discipline, as an element in human achievement? Was then Rousseau right to suggest that the *first* impulses of nature are always right? Is there not a flaw at the centre of romantic progressivism in its antagonism to restraints — an antagonism that would seem to be implicit in Read's definition of spontaneous expression as 'the unconstrained exteriorization of the mental activities of thinking, feeling, sensation and intuition'.[4]

Yet there are indications of a changed orientation in art education. I have over the years been examiner for two art education courses, one ten years ago, and one whose term of duty I have just finished. Technique and discipline are returning — 'spontaneity' in its primitive sense is out. The importance of tradition is being stressed by people like Hockney who are not really members of the avant-garde, and appears in the work of sculptors like Plazzotta. There is some sort of return to more traditional modes, techniques, disciplines.

VI

I hope now that the reason why I have spent so long on the Renaissance side will be becoming apparent because, by and large, I believe Renaissance aesthetic theory is much more soundly based than Romantic artistic theory.

The arts are ways of apprehending and exploiting reality — both that of the external world and that of the internal life. They are not to be regarded as peripheral or merely ornamental, nor do they necessarily arise out of an antagonistic attitude to society — that is at best a romantic half-truth. They do not result from esoteric movements nor are they constituted simply of the strange or the bizarre. Instead, they are central to us as human beings, because they are ways of exploring and apprehending the reality of our existence both in their internal manifestation of thoughts and feelings (it is important not to forget thoughts, for there are intellectual elements in all arts) and in our relations with the actual social and sensuous world around us.

I believe with Henry James that the province of art is all life, all feeling, all observation, all vision. But I also believe that the writers and artists of the Renaissance were right when they said that it was natural for human beings to be artificial. In artistic endeavour, what results is the outcome of discipline and effort, something made, not something that simply evolves, in some sense of that difficult word, 'naturally'. Art is a way of categorising the world but it exercises a *formative* element over that categorisation. This is, I think, one of the great realisations of Renaissance theorising: we inescapably *make* our lives. Erasmus was right when he urged, 'Homines non nascuntur sed finguntur' — 'men are not born, they are made.' They may be born with certain propensities — this the Renaissance admitted. But what one does with them is the result of human culture and human artifice and is not to be assigned to primitive impulse or impulse release. Hence in education what one is involved in is the creation of human beings in the course of an educative process. What I mean is very adequately summed up by a Renaissance literary theorist, Philip Sidney, when he implied that man, in the course of his development must 'grow into another nature'. He must transcend the primitive nature of the child or the baby and he must be formed through cultural artifice. This inevitably raises problems of value, for to be human is to be involved in the value dimension. (Indeed, what we argue about as being 'natural' is often simply a device for recommending an alternative set of values.) Part of that value dimension is what emerges out of the pain and effort of artistic creativity.

In this respect we ought to pay more attention to the Renaissance concept of 'imitation'. Imitation, as I have pointed out, involved the internalisation of aspects of past achievements, an essential element in creativity. We use this word 'creativity' carelessly and sometimes — though today perhaps less than we used to do — we seem to think that any manifestation of child behaviour if it's on paper somehow constitutes a manifestation of the creative. But, as our philosophers have pointed out, the essential element in the concept of creativity is some element of value; and therefore the Renaissance concept of 'imitation', with its notion of the internalisation of past models as essential elements in the creative process, seems to be a very fruitful one. I think that in schools we frequently give too much liberty to children to express themselves without giving them any of the tools with which they can discipline their expression. True, the Renaissance at its worst did the opposite. Renaissance theory at its most stultifying tended to stifle all originality and degenerate into copying. But the best of the Renaissance theorists realised this, and, as I have said, did not wish to turn their pupils into 'apes of Cicero'. They wished their artists to absorb the experience of the past in order to internalise it and to redeploy it in a genuine creative endeavour.

The view I am putting forward is very similar to the one expounded by Sir Ernst Gombrich in his book *Art and Illusion* where his famous remark 'making comes before matching' is to be found. By this he meant that in the development of artistic skill internalisation of schemata of previous artists comes before the actual copying of nature, that great artists have always acquired as much by 'imitation' of past models as they have from direct copying of nature. This surely is heavily influenced by Renaissance theory. As Henry James put it, the great thing is to be 'saturated' with something — and I don't think we 'saturate' our children enough. The urge to express must be balanced by the disciplined apprehension of the public symbols in terms of which expression acquires meaning.

91

Thus the arts involve the *control* as well as the *expression* of the emotions. I have written on this at some length in an essay published in my *Education, Culture and the Emotions*, and also in a little book *Culture, Industrialisation and Education*. Furthermore, educating the emotions means exploring aspects of emotional life which a child, without being involved in the work of others, without absorbing a great deal from the historical artefacts of his discipline, would not be introduced to: there are whole ranges of feeling which can only come as a result of *education*. Take for instance the notion of grace, *grazia* (a central concept in both the education of the Renaissance courtier and in the painting of pictures. Leonardo was reported to have *Divinia Grazia* divine grace.) Now such a notion, today, does not come 'naturally' through impulse release; it has to be learned. It is something which is acquired as a result of the study and internalisation of a sophisticated culture. And so the emotions seek expression but in the form of their expression need to be disciplined by an awareness of past forms. At the same time it is possible to introduce children to new ranges of emotions, aspects they are not familiar with in our emotionally vulgar age.

Then, again, I think the arts in education raise very crucial and important moral issues. I don't mean that art should be directly didactic, for instance by teaching morality through didactic types of poetry; but the revelation through art of various aspects of the reality of the world inevitably, to my mind, carries with it a value and moral dimension, and I consider the moral implications of the arts are extremely important and very central. Consider, for instance, the incidence of bad art, by which we are surrounded, and its potential for deleterious behaviour. One only has to turn a knob, and bad art is at one's command most hours of the day and night through radio and television – and this is the art that most people absorb from their environment. The whole question and role of bad art in our society needs very careful consideration. Clearly it requires an article on its own, and it can only be raised here as an issue implicit in this crucially important matter of values. Arts of a sort are not neglected in our society; never has there been a time when there has been more art; one can get various types of dramas and plays almost any moment of the day and night one likes to turn one's television on. Yet so much of this art is of a very inferior and inadequate nature. In this respect, this indictment by Professor Susanne Langer conveys the essence of my meaning:[5]

> People who are so concerned for their children's scientific
> enlightenment that they keep Grimm out of the library and Santa
> Claus out of the chimney allow the cheapest art, the worst of bad
> singing, the most revolting sentimental fiction to impinge on the

children's minds all day and every day from infancy. If the rank and file of youth grows up in emotional cowardice and confusion, sociologists look to economic conditions or family relations for the cause of this deplorable human weakness but not to the ubiquitous influence of corrupt art, which steeps the average mind in a shallow sentimentalism that ruins what germs of true feeling might have developed in it.

I should like to add a final point on the subject-matter of children's art in its extended meaning. So often in current artistic creativity in schools and colleges, whether it be writing or painting, dance, etc., children and students will seek out the esoteric. This also constitutes an aspect of romanticism: they seem to want to explore the pathological or the odd or the distant, the remote or the fantastic. They write about cops and robbers – not perhaps quite so remote these days, but few of them have actually had any experience of such matters. Indeed, they don't write about them as if from actual experience, they write as if they had picked it up from the latest soap opera on the television. Again, students when they are doing their dances, often tend either to choose vast cosmic themes which they cannot in fact cope with or some quasi-pathological subject-matter. They are very much bound up with certain pathological elements in our society.

But why seek the extraordinary? Why not try to explore and transmute the ordinary, the everyday? There is in this connection a marvellous remark by Chekov. Chekov was given a short story by a friend to read. He encountered a long passage of description about the moonlight, which at interminable length described it in all its aspects. Chekov wrote back to his friend and said: 'Cut out all those pages about the moonlight, give us instead what you feel about it – the reflection of the moon in a piece of broken bottle.' That image – 'the reflection of the moon in a piece of broken bottle' – sums up for me this notion of the ability of the great, the really creative, artist to transmute the very ordinary. Moonlight and broken bottle, commonplaces of our experience – but the combination of the two sums up this ability of the artist to take the real, the everyday, the mundane, and transform it by making it symbolic of a larger whole. Some such power of compression, of transmuting the ordinary elements of real life, would prevent some of those poems which one sees too often on the walls of classrooms or the dances which too often I have to witness or the paintings of fantasy. (There may be a place for fantasy but it must be a controlled fantasy – one which gets to the essence of a situation. Some of the best examples of controlled fantasy are to be found in our fairy-tales – which, as Bruno Bettelheim has pointed out, are geared to certain fundamental realities of the human situation.)[6] Let us then try to avoid those ridiculous fantasies children indulge in — about Batman, for instance, or Superman or fantasies of a sort which make no contact with the realities of human life. After all, art will only help children come to terms with reality if we encourage them to exercise themselves on their real feelings and sensations of the world around them. In this way the arts can remain important centres of human endeavour, means through which men are enabled to make something of themselves — for remember 'men are not born, but made'. In the same way the arts don't arise as a result of untutored spontaneity, impulse release, but through the internalisation of past models of greatness and the disciplined approach to creativity this involves.

Chapter 6

The death of Bazarov

Student movements are part of nineteenth-century as well as of twentieth-century history, and some of their perennially characteristic features may be gleaned from one of the great classic studies of the inter-generational conflict, Turgenev's *Fathers and Sons*. So much is this the case, indeed, that Professor Lewis S. Feuer in his monumental study of the character and significance of student movements, *The Conflict of Generations*, refers to his own analysis of the Russian student movement as 'a series of footnotes to Ivan Turgenev's immortal *Fathers and Sons*; we can only try to transcribe into sociological prose what this novelist's genius perceived at the very beginning of the movement.'[1]

In Bazarov, then, the protagonist of the novel, we see a type of the disaffected student — disaffected, that is to say, with the older generation and all its works, for inter-generational conflict is an essential ingredient in all student movements — caught up in the actualities of specific social situations and moral dilemmas. We see him as leader — albeit with a single disciple, Arkady; we see him as critic, as he lays down the law to the older generation at Arkady's house; but we also see him as 'victim' — of the very social and emotional forces which his student credo bids him repudiate. One of these is love. This he thinks he can easily 'place': 'For of what do the so-called mysterious relations between a man and a woman consist? As physiologists, we know precisely of what they consist.'[2]

It is not surprising, then, to hear such a man proclaim that 'A good chemist is worth a score of your poets.'[3] Alas for human arrogance! Madame Odintsov teaches him that the inside of a man is rather more complicated than that of a frog, to which, earlier in the book, he has, with a sublime impertinence, compared the human being:[4]

'For what do you want frogs, *barin*' asked one of the lads.
'To make them useful' replied Bazarov ... 'You see, I like to open
them, and then to observe what their insides are doing. You and I
are frogs too, except that we walk upon our hind legs. Thus the
operation helps me to understand what is taking place in ourselves.'

On his deathbed, his anti-romanticism — romanticism is one of the
gravest crimes with which he accuses the older generation — finally
disappears. His cool reductionism ('love is a mere empirical sentiment'),
which he strives to maintain until the last moment as he continues (in
his final talk with Madame Odintsov) to analyse his state of mind and
his attitude to his own death, breaks down as the feeling she engenders
seizes him and leads to an outburst of emotion:[5]

> But what did I want to say to you? That I have loved you? There
> was a time when the phrase 'I love' had for me no meaning; and
> now it will have less than ever, seeing that love is a form, and
> that my particular embodiment of it is fast lapsing towards
> dissolution. It — Ah, how perfect you are! You stand there as
> beautiful as —

The case which Bazarov represents may be generalised: student
revolt against their 'fathers' stems from a grossly over-simplified view of
the human condition. Here, however, I must break off to point out
that, implicit in the movement for student power, there are two broad
categories of desiderata. One relates to practicalities relevant to the life
of a student — his work, examinations, lodgings and the like. About
these he may be said to have a certain amount of insight, in the same
sort of way that a trade unionist may be said to have knowledge and
understanding relevant to his specific calling. Here, then, the demands
of the students are likely to be controlled, to some extent at least, by
a sense of reality. Their demands may be excessive or impracticable, but
they are not usually without the bounds of possibility, and they can be
countered in typical unionist manner by bargaining. I shall refer to
student demands of this type as 'unionist'.

But it is frequent for claims of this sort to be contained within a
larger framework, when the whole social structure comes under criticism and attack. Here the aims are apocalyptic and millenarian, nothing
other, indeed, than the transformation of the social order itself. There
is always the likelihood, of course, that the more specific and restricted
aims will coalesce with more utopian purposes, and quite usual that the
motive power behind specific demands will gain impetus from strongly
held but essentially imprecise charges of corruption and inadequacy
against the larger society. In so far as the conflict is basically inter-
generational — and Professor Feuer's analysis on this point seems

irrefutable, i.e. conscious and unconscious rejection of the father seems to play a determinate role in the conflict – then it is not surprising that the emotion of rejection should define itself in characteristic refutations of the inevitably imperfect features of the social order within which the students find themselves and for which the older generation can be held responsible. The unmistakable grain of justification in the rejection will not be counter-balanced by any appreciation of the essential element of equivocation demanded by the complexity of human affairs and the dilemmas implicit in any social 'solution' arrived at on the basis of even the highest moral purposes. That even moral principles may clash is not a point likely to be taken by young people who still see the world in essentially simplistic terms. Only wider 'experience' than they can as yet command will reveal the compromises necessary in the realistic pursuit of even the purest of aims; they do not as yet appreciate the truth that all good men do not necessarily pursue compatible ends.

One way of achieving enlightenment is through developments in the self, through the realisation that one may well have been mistaken in one's own positive and not fully acknowledged aspirations. Hence the role in the novel of Arkady, the faithful disciple. Arkady, who is shown in the earlier part of the book as a faithful echo of his master's voice, accepts the enlargement of experience which is implicit in his love for Katia. He says to her, in the scene in which he declares his affection for her:[6]

> though I still wish to be of use in life, though I still wish to consecrate the whole of my faculties to the service of Truth, I no longer seek my ideals where I was wont to do – they appear to me to stand much nearer home. Hitherto I have been in ignorance of myself, hitherto I have set myself tasks beyond my powers; but now, through a certain feeling which is within me, my eyes have become opened.

'I have been in ignorance of myself': this frankness compares interestingly with Bazarov's claim to have so dissected the human mind as to have discovered all its secrets. Human beings are not so easily analysed.

And here, indeed, it might be worth taking a brief look at the terms in which this analysis has been attempted by the youthful rebel. It is not an accident that Bazarov is shown to be a scientist – of sorts; not indeed, a scientist in the sense of one who suspends judgment until he has noted carefully the facts, but as one who has exploited a dogmatism to which the scientific outlook may appear to lend itself when 'explanations' are offered which provide easy or at least manageable solutions to the complexity of life's emotional problems. Bazarov's philosophy could be criticised in much the same terms as W.B. Yeats applied to

George Bernard Shaw's: 'It seemed to me inorganic, logical straightness and not the crooked road of life.' Science, indeed, in the nineteenth century was likely to be attractive to a generation in revolt. For one thing it was essentially a discipline where change usually was progress; furthermore, it could offer forms of reductionism, simplifying formulae in terms of which life's mysteries could be made comprehensible. A scientific approach applied a single criterion of judgment; it was both annihilistic and reconstructive, reducing all experience to a single criterion of relevance and yet filling the emotional gap which a total nihilism would necessarily leave.

The natural sciences since the seventeenth century have implied the categorisation of 'experience' into primary and secondary qualities; what then became 'real' were the abstract formulations derived from the selective study of certain aspects of phenomena. As Gerard Manley Hopkins, who was himself a literary artist intensely interested in science (he actually published in *Nature*), put it:[7]

> The study of physical science has, unless corrected in some way, an effect the very opposite of what one would suppose. One would think it might materialize people . . . but in fact they seem to end in conceiving only a world of formulas, with its being properly speaking in thought . . . .

Furthermore, in the nineteenth century this 'world of formulas' carried with it the immense prestige of a still comparatively young set of disciplines which seemed to be laying open the secrets of the universe. Today's natural scientists are morally rather more unsure than those of the nineteenth century about the ultimate outcome of their discoveries. Something of their former naive confidence in having solved the riddles of the world has been taken over by the social scientists – which is perhaps why the latter are now much more prominent in student protest than the natural scientists, who, in England at least, are generally quiescent.

But in the nineteenth century natural science reduced the bewildering qualitative differentiations of life into terms comprehensible to inexperience. After all, if love is nothing but chemistry it has become 'placed' and therefore manageable: one is able to observe oneself in relationship, but in no sense required to submit oneself in exploration of one's most intimate personal experience. If all principles are to be questioned which cannot be empirically demonstrated (which is the essence of Bazarov's nihilism) then one can remain apart from the tangle of actual social values and relationships, perhaps to favour abstract ones from which the pressures of immediate living have been removed. Hence the curious sense of isolation which characterises Bazarov's relations with the other characters in the novel (today it is termed 'alienation'); it is most marked in his contempt for the older generation and their suspicions about his lack of commitment and principle, about his desire to deny everything. 'First must the site be cleared,' he proclaims as his guiding principle for social regeneration. The issue becomes clear in his initial conversation with Paul Petrovitch, Arkady's uncle. Paul Petrovitch accuses him:[8]

Have you ever considered *what* you are maintaining with your miserable creed? . . . 'A force, forsooth'. You might as well say that the wild Kulmak, or the barbaric Mongol, represents a force. What boots such a force? Civilisation and its fruits are what we value. And do not tell me that those fruits are to be overlooked, seeing that even the meanest scribbler, the meanest piano-player who ever earned five kopeks a night, is of more use to society than you. For men of that kind at least stand for culture rather than for some rude, Mongolian propelling-power.

The point does not go home, and shortly after Bazarov seeks to end the conversation by asserting: 'Whenever you may feel that you can point out to me a single institution in our family or our public life which does not call for complete and unsparing rejection, I shall be pleased to accept your view.'[9]

Before we examine the implications of the final outcome of the novel — the death of Bazarov — and its relevance to the analysis of Bazarov's position so far made, it is necessary to apply Turgenev's insights to our contemporary Bazarovs. One notes the same sense of the overwhelming importance of contradiction rather than affirmation. Bazarov has some positive aspirations for national regeneration, which he expresses in terms of usefulness — the need for food and certain manifestations of material prosperity. But the overwhelming impression is one of bitter criticism:[10]

that beyond question are our so-called leaders and censors not worth their salt, seeing that they engage in sheer futilities, and waste their breath on discussions on art and still life and Parliamentarianism and legal points and the devil only knows what, when all the time it is the bread of subsistence alone that matters. . . .

In the same way, current student movements of the millenarian variety are much more categorical about what they are against than about what they are for. In general they tend to be against much of what Bazarov is against — though in the contemporary idiom this translates itself into a rejection of the 'Establishment' or the 'System'. It is not an accident, either, that as I have already briefly indicated, social scientists, especially sociologists, appear to be prominent among the protestors. Bazarov, as we have seen, puts his faith in the sciences — in his case, natural sciences.

But the social as well as the natural sciences can become shields against the complexities of life. To reduce the world to 'thought', cognition, 'a world of formulas', is the achievement of both in their different spheres. Sociology, for instance, depends on the assumption that social phenomena, social actions, though they necessarily manifest themselves in the consciousness of individuals, can yet be regarded as so similar in nature as to permit classification as regularities. To put it another way, sociology depends on the assumption which I have expressed elsewhere as the 'democracy of shared perspectives';[11] so what I see or do and what my neighbour sees or does can be regarded as sufficiently alike as to enable their detachment as phenomena and their subsumption under general categories.

These characteristic features of what is most 'modern', 'relevant' (and therefore appealing) in the curriculum, together with the will to power encouraged by modern technology as part of the very atmosphere of the world they inhabit, will go some way to explaining the phenomenon we call 'student power'. For student power is something more than simply the ebullience of youth which, say, disturbed the streets of Verona in the days of the Capulets and the Montagues. The phenomenon of student power rests on a conscious ideology of self-assertion manifest in certain primarily cognitive judgments which display all the characteristics of 'a world of formulas', in Hopkins's sense of the phrase, and therefore unchecked by contact with the irreducible contingencies and pressures of everyday living. The student world is after all a world in which certain demands are not made on the individual – he does not have to earn a living, he lives in a protected environment. Furthermore, it is a world in which the characteristic thought forms, whatever the subject of study, are towards the abstract and the selective. Thus the way is open for such claims and manifestations as we have recently seen in the West and which many countries have suffered ever since the nineteenth century. It was the genius of Turgenev to have appreciated much of this.

I am in no way asserting that these are the sole factors which foster the claims of student power. Indeed, alone they would not necessarily be sufficient. Professor Feuer is surely correct to urge that a major factor in nearly all student outbreaks is what he terms the 'de-authoritization' of the older generation. In some way the young come no longer to respect the older generation; often it is because the middle aged are too permissive and 'liberal'. This offends against the absolutism which tends to mark the outlook of the intelligent young, and reminds us of the accuracy of T.S. Eliot's diagnosis when he described liberalism as 'a movement not so much defined by its end, as by its starting point; away from rather than towards something definite. Our point of departure is more real to us than our destination.'

The liberal spirit is in general inimical to the spirit of youth because it is characterised by tolerance, self-awareness and a capacity for self-criticism which in general young people often do not possess. And it also means that the liberally minded tend to be less certain in their view of the future, less certain in directive. Liberalism at its best implies the 'free play of mind', and this is at odds with the certainty and dogmatism which the over-simplifications of youth encourage. Hence liberalism itself is often regarded by the young as the enemy. The New Radicals recently defined the aims of what they call the Movement in these terms: 'The Movement rejects the careers and life styles of the American liberal . . . for to the Movement it is the liberal way of life and frame of mind that represent the evil of America.'[12] Hence, too, initially at least, the young have the advantage of certainty and tend to gain their own way. This can be illustrated by what has too often been the fate of the universities. Almost by definition the universities are the homes of the liberal spirit; above all else the university stands for the spirit of free inquiry and the suspension of judgment. It is an institution intended almost by nature to be attacked by the young – in so far, that is, as its members adhere to the university's traditional values.

It is true that students in their demands often seem to exploit the liberalism of the university by pushing such liberalism to its logical conclusion – to anarchy, that is, which is the dogmatism implicit in the liberal spirit. For true liberalism can distinguish itself from licence, whereas the dogmatism of liberalism cannot. The notion of limitation is implicit in the very ambiguities of freedom – in the distinction between 'freedom from' and 'freedom to'. Experience goes to show that boundaries can create positive opportunities as well as inhibit possibilities. One cannot just live; it is necessary to live in certain terms, and the terms always imply the abandonment of possibilities which lie outside their boundaries. No one can ever exploit all his potentialities; it is always necessary to choose and to concentrate in order to permit the release of powers. But this is beyond the purview of the young, who see in liberty only a release from restriction. Hence, paradoxically, the young exploit and pervert the spirit of liberalism in order to attack it.

It should by now have become apparent that what I am attempting is the definition of conditions which are peculiarly propitious for the student manifestations we have witnessed in recent years. It is only in the nineteenth century that the formal system of education through school and university begins to get the edge on the informal system of private tutor, Grand Tour and the like, on which the elite of the country had long been nurtured. It is when the spirit of the university needs to be taken seriously that we begin to get the first outbursts of student disorder and aspiration. In other words, there is something about the ethos of the university which lays itself open to the sorts of events with which this essay is concerned. For one thing, the very liberalism of the university provides some measure of that de-authoritisation which has been recognised as a prime element in the manifestation of moves to install student power. But there is more to it than that. The learning which the university provides encourages knowledge (which is power) without experience or responsibility. All too easily, then, does it encourage (as, admittedly, a perversion of its action) the simplifying formula, the abstraction untested in concrete actuality. Even in the greater world the specialisation which the university encourages implies the brutality of minds that know a great deal about a little and not much about anything else. Ally this to the characteristic features of youth and its patent lack of experience and the way is open for crude and simplistic manifestations of self-assertion, justifying themselves by crude 'ideas' from which are removed all the actual emotional pressures of real life.

It is interesting to note, however, the way in which student leaders, once faced with the actualities of everyday life, often become themselves pillars of the Establishment which previously they had been all too ready to attack. In Japan, for instance, there is considerable competition among industrial firms to recruit some of the more militant student activists on the grounds that, once integrated into the companies, they become aggressive models of good executives and salesmen. A similar phenomenon was noted by Bernard Pares in 1907, when he commented on the way in which the Russian bureaucratic system succeeded in integrating student activists once more into the community. In Russia, nearly everyone was directly or indirectly an official. Faced with the need to earn a living, the student 'has hardly any choice except either to take a great many things as he finds them or to set himself against the whole system of society.' Clearly few have either the training or the moral courage to do the latter, once they have left the comfort of their like-minded companions and have entered the great world. Hence the rapid disappearance of activism; indeed, Pares comments: 'The evidence of all my informants goes to show that those students who have shouted loudest against the Government become the most submissive and self-seeking officials.'[13] As Moissaye J. Olgin, who participated in demonstrations in Kiev in 1900 and became a leading Communist editor in the United States later pointed out, the ordinary biography of a Russian intellectual followed a pattern of revolutionary activism followed by reintegration into the community:[14]

> at twenty, an ardent revolutionist (in theory) repudiating
> compromises (in discussions with his friends), cherishing the most
> novel social ideals; at twenty-five, a county physician, or a teacher
> ... trying to be progressive and human, and being handicapped at

every step by the bureaucratic machinery . . .; at thirty, a 'tired' man, exhausted by the unequal struggle, disgusted by his failures . . .; at thirty-five, a moral wreck, assimilated by his environment beyond recognition. . . .

It was the genius of Turgenev to recognise this situation forty years earlier; for symbolically this is what the death of Bazarov implied. Professor Feuer adduces Bazarov's demise as instancing the self-destructive, suicidal element involved in adolescent student movements. It may well be that there is a hint of this, but the incident is surely open to another interpretation. Bazarov returns to his father's house; at first he isolated himself in order to work, but after a time he ceases to closet himself. There follow fits of depression and ennui:

from his gait there disappeared its old firm, active self-confidence, and ceasing to indulge in solitary rambles, he took to cultivating society, to attending tea in the drawing room, to pacing the kitchen garden, and to joining Vasili Ivanitch in a silent smoking of pipes.

It is a short step from this to becoming his father's partner, assisting in the medical care of the surrounding peasantry.

In fine, what we have is the disintegration of the nihilist, scoffing at all mundane daily happenings, the enemy of ordinary domesticity. Bazarov continues to scoff in words, but his actions begin to indicate the beginnings of the process of integration into the very life of the community that intellectually he rejects. He can no longer maintain his 'alienation' – and so the nihilist must die. Symbolically Turgenev makes him die as a result of the very act of dissection – though in this case the body of a typhus victim is involved – which until recently he had urged as a means of discovering the mysteries of life, through his dissection of frogs. The science by which he has sought to live, has, unwittingly, led to his death. But his death arises really because ultimately he cannot resist the claims which even what he regards as a corrupt society make upon him.

So in the death of Bazarov we find symbolised the falling away which almost inevitably afflicts the activist once he has been forced to face up to the inevitability of his relationships with the larger community. Turgenev gives poetic expression – realises it in its full emotional context – to the tale which Olgin tells of the life history of a typical student activist. The demands and needs of society carry on as before. Student activism at trade union level can lead to certain reforms; the food and the lectures may improve because the intervention may to some extent at least spring out of direct knowledge and understanding. Even here some of the 'benefits' may prove to be equivocal. Not all students are capable of coming to wise decisions even about what most nearly and intimately concerns them; what, for instance, they may consider good lecturing may, on closer inspection, hardly warrant the attribution. Too easily are they taken in by the glib and the merely entertaining.

But where the wider society is concerned, their interventions are nearly always disastrous. However ostensibly virtuous their aims may be, however apparently concerned with the poor and the oppressed, the methods the activists employ imply that the broader society must resist in order to protect itself. The danger, then, is the backlash – which historically has often occurred. Nor is it possible to condemn society for its reaction. For, as Mr Harry Kidd has pointed out, 'there is much which is very dangerous in the student approach':[15]

> There is a rejection of the patient, practical, virtues of pragmatism and compromise as hypocritical. There is a belief that blind adherence to 'principles' is in all circumstances right, as if sincerity (the quintessence of which is fanaticism) were the one political virtue; as if principles were never in conflict; as if it were better to do much harm for good motives than to be realistically content with doing some modest good.

Yet, of course, to ask for these virtues is to ask, in general, for what the young find most difficult, by nature, to provide. For to aim at *modest* good is to have taken the world's measure in a way which is beyond all but the most mature of the young; and to see that 'principles' may conflict is to have had experience of the manifestations of 'principles' in concrete actuality which the average 20-year-old is unlikely to have achieved. The student acquires his 'principles' as 'ideas', with all the abstraction from emotional reality which this implies. He cannot be expected to have written *Fathers and Sons* before he is old enough to appreciate its firm grasp on the actual complexities of living.

Nevertheless, in the nineteenth and twentieth centuries what is essentially a new situation has arisen. The universities have moved to the centre of the educational process – no merely informal system can now compete. The education they provide is primarily cognitive – it pays little attention to the education of the emotions. 'Ideas' are often explosive – and frequently inadequate to the living organic, experience of men.[16] Furthermore, university dons can no longer rely on the traditional respect accorded, in the past, to age and superior knowledge.

Here lies the educational value of what I have termed the 'unionist' issues, if only they are properly handled by the university authorities. There is nothing so calming to revolutionary ardour as the concrete exploration of specific issues in all their complexities and ramifications. Any university professor who has sat on a number of committees knows in the vast majority of issues how small the area of manoeuvrability in fact is. Student 'participation' at this level, then, might well be thought a very salutary experience, somewhat analogous to what takes place when student activists actually find themselves part of the larger community. Only by patient consideration of all the relevant *facts* can wise *value* decisions be arrived at. The wilder flights of revolutionary aspiration have historically nearly always led to disaster – to a situation indeed worse than might have occurred had the revolution not advertised itself. Temporary success has led to ultimate failure. A genuine opportunity for insight into the processes which are necessary for decision-making would have been the positive virtues of providing a good training in the possibilities of change for adult life and thus obviating the tragic waste of time and effort of intelligent young people which their current obsession with and naive concern for political issues involves. If students can be brought to realise how difficult it is to bring about change within a restricted social framework, how 'reform' itself frequently carries with it an equivocal air when it is seen in practice, the enthusiasm of all but the revolutionary hard-liners might be quenched and they might be brought to a greater sense of social reality and therefore social usefulness.

In other words, what I am advocating is a university lead in 'unionist' politics; that concessions should not be wrung from a reluctant administration, but that it should be regarded as a desirable part of the university education of the politically active students that they should see something of decision-making at first hand. Let me make it quite clear that I still regard this very much as university 'paternalism'. Whatever happens, the 'fathers' must not abdicate their responsibilities; they must merely seek to exercise them in a wiser way – by a positive educational programme (which, after all is their business) rather than by a reluctant concession. For the latter simply betrays the uncertainty and weakness into which the 'fathers' have fallen. It should be appreciated that the revolt against the fathers is always, in the last resort, equivocal. Apart from the criminal few, the basic psychological cry is as much 'Why don't you stop me' as 'Let me have what I want.' Wise fathers, it seems to me, must learn to seek solutions which mix the two; at the same time, they must accept their responsibilities as fathers. None are more pathetic in university circles than those arrested adolescents among the staff who regress to the level of the student activists. Rightly does a university take a stand against such men. At the same time it must be recognised that we live in an age of heightened awareness – to which the young are as much subjected as anyone else. The times call for new *educational* solutions and not either repression or regression. Something of this has happened, but in the uneasy spirit of our times concessions are continually being sought after: it is essential to think out the principles in terms of which these can be met. For, as in the 1980s the times get harder, it is impossible not to think that further challenges will appear.

Chapter 7

Equality and education

I

The concept of 'equality' inevitably arouses notions of 'sameness' or 'similarity'; the dictionary defines 'equal' as being of the same in quality, degree, merit, etc. The movement towards equality in social terms can be charted as manifest in the growth of specific 'samenesses' or similarities institutionalised in the social structure of the community. What starts as a bare awareness of a common humanity recognised as operative in little else except the grave —

> Sceptre and crown
> Shall tumble down
> And in the grave be equal laid
> With the poor crooked scythe and spade

— gradually takes on increasing customary and legalistic substance. In education, for instance, we start when all must go to school; we move on to the time when all must be provided with secondary school, then that all should go to the same sort of secondary school. Further refinements of equality are introduced when it is suggested that all should undertake a common curriculum, even a common syllabus, for at least a length of time. Then it is urged that the school shall be organised in such a way that each form should contain a roughly similar range of ability. Here the aim is a common experience to produce the similarity of understanding thought relevant to a democratic community. Even the way in which the curriculum is transmitted may be affected. Where the order and continuity of subject-matter is concerned John Dewey considered that[1]

> The basic control resides in the nature of the situations in which the young take part. In social situations the young have to refer

their way of acting to what others are doing and make it fit in. This directs their action to a common result, and gives an understanding common to the participants. For all *mean* the same thing, even when performing different acts.

Yet here surely we are pulled up short. Notions of consciousness and the meanings which accompany consciousness are central to the whole task of Western formal education. Education, in this sense, is concerned with the handing on of such part of the cultural heritage as is responsive to formal transmission — as a matter, that is, of conscious transaction between teacher and taught. These parts of the cultural heritage are manifest as collections of significances, modes of understanding, skilled activities and the like — 'meanings' in a broad sense — which require for their successful assimilation particularised orientations on the part of the pupil. To have introjected in any significant sense one of these 'meanings' is to have achieved an inwardness with specific concepts and their interrelationships, styles of argument, data, etc., to a degree which is usually in some measure publicly testable in ways which are likely to reveal defined gradations of understanding. Externally, in terms of school provision and organisation, it may be possible to produce at least superficial impressions of sameness or at least similarity. But when we get to the very core of the educational process, we need to ask to what extent it is possible to agree that all in fact do *mean* the same thing in either their actions or their understanding. Put it another way, as cultural meaning extends in depth, range and subtlety, to what extent can it be argued that all can share equally in the full range of meanings implicit in the formal curriculum of the schools? For this is the central issue which faces those who through organisational manipulation would seem to seek to produce at least an appearance of a common submission to an equivalent experience. It is with this issue that we are ultimately concerned in any discussion of educational equality.

II

One important effect of the eighteenth-century Enlightenment was to substitute an abstract vision of the earthly perfectibility of humanity for the old historical Christian view of fallen man and the effort necessary for the attainment of grace. Basically, the new view was anti-historical, though in fact it often drew on a series of carefully selected historical examples to support its apocalyptic vision, often those drawn from the supposed nature of a primitive society. It was anti-historical, however, in the sense that it laid the blame for human shortcomings on the historical situation in current society, and postulated human regeneration through a manipulation of the human environment which would permit a fresh start – perhaps through preserving an original innocence, as in *Emile*. Naturally the easiest way of manipulating this environment would seem to be through education. As Helvetius expressed it: 'l'éducation nous faisait ce que nous sommes'; manifest differences of attainment were to be blamed on the circumstances in which men were placed and especially on the particular form of the political system and government under which they existed. Genius was common, but it needed extraordinary conditions to bring it out – 'il est beaucoup d'appelés et peu d'élus.' A characteristic twentieth-century theme was already in process of formulation and promulgation. Locke and indeed Quintilian before him had already advanced the proposition that inequality in minds resulted from differences in education; though at that time much the more usual view was that a 'natural' hierarchy existed which was reflected in the diversity of social rank and roles, arising out of disparities of birth and that virtuous conduct which was supposed to be the justification of aristocracy. A combination of circumstances which, on other grounds, focused on the importance of education helped to make Locke's proposition more widely acceptable than it had previously been, though even then its full force was not appreciated until nearly our own times in the world of practical educational politics.

Yet, at the same time that the role of education was receiving increasing theoretical emphasis, the beginnings of great social and structural changes in Western society consequent upon scientific, technological and industrial development produced the specific social conditions which enabled theoretical speculation to feed into practical policies. The educational revolution of the Renaissance period had instigated the important notion that men of government (the courtier, the governor) needed also to be men of education; and so the comparatively mindless chivalric ideal of the Middle Ages was fused, during the early Tudor period, with the Italian humanistic model derived from classical antiquity to form a new conception of a ruling aristocracy.

The curriculum, however, remained broadly classical, despite periodical attempts to widen it and make it more relevant to developing mercantile and commercial interests. Even with the accelerating technological and scientific needs of the later eighteenth and nineteenth centuries, the classical curriculum retained much of its prestige down almost to our own times. Nevertheless, in reality, great changes had already taken place by the beginning of the twentieth century, as the ideal of the classically educated, 'amateur' gentleman began to seem increasingly irrelevant to the rapidly developing demands of industry and of the industrial and governmental bureaucracies which accompanied industrialisation. The net effect of these changes was to create a new socially inspired image of the acceptable educated man, that of the expert. Growing technical demands of differing sorts necessitated the production of an increasingly functional elite, one capable of supplying the specific demands implicit in the new fragmented technological order. The older conception of the essentially amateur if knowledgeable man of affairs was increasingly challenged by the newer professionalism.

The implications of all this for education I will spell out shortly. It is relevant to point out, however, that the technological and scientific developments which have been alluded to above have been accompanied, inevitably, by social and political changes which are of the greatest importance for my theme. The great watershed here is the French Revolution and the destruction of the *ancien regime* which resulted. The net result of this essentially political move was the breakdown of a whole network of traditional allegiances: 'In our days,' as de Tocqueville wrote, 'men see that the constituted powers are crumbling down on every side; they see all ancient authority dying out, all ancient barriers tottering to their fall, and the judgement of the wisest is troubled at the sight.' The net result at the lower levels, for instance, was to prise the labourer out of his traditional framework and redeploy him at the mercy of the market as a 'hand'. The consequence was both liberation (of a sort) and atomisation – but the ground was being prepared for a degree of upward and downward mobility unknown to former times. Furthermore, the concept of social class entered into our social and political thinking, and the old conception of traditional hierarchy based on the notion of a 'chain of being' was replaced by the idea of stratification on class lines. Part of the significance of the difference lies in the opportunity afforded to think of the new status differentiation of class as the product of the play of social forces rather than as an unquestionable characteristic of the social order. Another of the profound legacies of the eighteenth-century Enlightenment and of the Revolution which concluded it was the belief that the social order, like the natural order, was subject to human manipulation.

If these two legacies of the Enlightenment and of the cataclysm in which it culminated are brought into relationship with the movement towards the perfectibility of man noted in my opening remarks, the scene is set for some sort of questioning of the inequalities of the new class differentiation which was replacing the old traditional hierarchic organisation. As Professor Robert Nisbet has pointed out in *The Sociological Tradition*, there were, broadly speaking, two attitudes which developed towards the new stratified system. One of these attitudes saw the new stratification in terms of a reproduction, in the new industrial order, of the old pre-industrial rigidities; the other posited a much more fluid system, 'a scrambling of social categories to an individualisation of stratification which would result in the ascendancy not of class but of social status – which is at once more mobile, individually autonomous, and diversified than class.'[2] As Professor Nisbet warns, the contrast must not be over-emphasised; neither group of thinkers was oblivious of class in some form or other. But the one saw it as a rigid, solidified series of strata; the other as something more flexible, shifting and subject to the play of the market.

Now these two views of the nature of the developing industrial order are likely to assign somewhat differing roles to education. It is true that they will not have been as explicitly formulated at the time as they appear in Professor Nisbet's analysis; rather they constitute summations of attitudes drawn up with the advantages of hindsight. Nevertheless, one can see that even without full conscious realisation of the logic of their positions, holders of each view are likely to differ in their attitudes to equality and in their views of how one of the tools which might help to bring it about, education, should be employed. Their differing approaches may be revealed in their diversified handling of the notion of equality of opportunity. Those who stress the fluidity of society are likely to advocate equality of opportunity as contributing to this fluidity. Approaching the problems of the developing industrial-bureaucratic stage pragmatically, they are likely to be impressed with the need to develop many of the new skills which society is going to require through education, and to advocate an increasingly open society, affording opportunities for status differentiation to individuals as both a means of satisfying the new restless aspirations of various sections of the developing social order and as a means of feeding the new demands of industrialisation. So great are these latter that it becomes necessary to call upon sections of the community hitherto depressed to provide some of the new recruits, on the assumption that there may be concealed among them a small reservoir of talent which, given an opportunity, may provide the necessary expertise for the new order.

Hence there develops the idea of the 'ladder of opportunity'. A more equal exposure to the life chances provided by education would enable children of talent from the lower classes to take their places in the higher levels of power in the new social order which was evolving; indeed, without these new recruitments it would hardly be possible to sustain the new society. Thus the equality implied was one at the starting-post – a more equal opportunity to become unequal, as it were. Mobility was possible, desirable and should be assisted. As the society developed there was seen to be an ever growing need for talent, and so 'opportunity' was slowly increased. At the same time, there has been increasing pressure in the twentieth century to provide the rest of the population with an education suitable to their capacities and needs, so that the further implication of the equalising process becomes one of providing education which is *equally appropriate but different*. This solution to the problems of equality which had been inherited from the eighteenth century I will term the 'meritocratic' one. We were to take advantage of the fluidity which had been diagnosed as the characteristic feature of the new industrialisation by reinforcing it by education. Indeed, educational attainment became a chief criterion by which the new mobility could be implemented.

Educationally speaking, the chief consequence of this approach was, initially, the setting up of a new universal system of schooling, the chief curriculum requirement of which was cognitive in orientation. The latter point is important because it provided a curriculum which, in many of its manifestations, could be assimilated, given the necessary cognitive ability, by the culturally unsophisticated. An inwardness with the old humanistic culture with its many-faceted artistic and literary implications depended as much on a process of slow assimilation as on conscious instruction. Those who achieved most were those who participated in the way of life to which this culture was native. The historical inadequacy, bordering in some cases on gross incompetence, of the instruction in many of the schools and universities was therefore not a matter of such vital importance, though it was not a matter of total indifference either. But there were other informal ways through which the necessary knowledge and, more importantly, taste, could be acquired. Ideally, the introduction was not simply into the ways of knowing characteristic of the classical culture, but into its ways of feeling also – and the latter was not something which could necessarily be best transmitted through schooling.

But the new curriculum with its concentration on positive knowledge, its emphasis on science and on the semi-scientific subjects, like geography, and its comparative neglect of the arts and literature (literature, when it appeared, often occurred as subject-matter for grammatical exercise) could be much more easily assimilated through the processes of formal instruction. In view of criticisms which I will raise later of the whole meritocratic implication, it is important to bear this in mind.

For the moment, however, I wish to return to consider the implications, for the implementation of the notion of equality, of the other view of social stratification – that which saw it as mere translation, into nineteenth-century terms, of the old rigidities of the pre-industrial agricultural society. This evoked a much more revolutionary response. The tendency now is to use education as a device, a tool by which these rigidities can be overthrown and a more equal and therefore desirable society produced. It is therefore no longer a question of equality at the starting-line, but rather at the finishing-post; the means to this is *sameness* of provision. This I will refer to as the 'egalitarian' solution. Clearly the stubborn irreducible facts of human differentiation, however explained, make it difficult to maintain this view in practice for long, but as an ideal it has exercised a certain influence on the specific educational provisions of certain nations in recent years. Thus for quite a time the Soviet system retained a mass element as its defining characteristic. The aim here was not to use education as a selective sieve for catching the ablest and discarding the rest; the stress, in the earlier years of the Soviet system, was on 'providing a basic general education, covering the same ground and on the same terms for all, regardless of background or future occupation'.[3] Hence equality comes to imply sameness in experiential terms. In this, of course, it is only in line with Marxist-Leninist ideology, where the paramount emphasis is on the building of a communist society and on the use of education as a tool to that end. 'Without teaching there is no knowledge,' Lenin once remarked, 'and without knowledge there is no communism.' Initial differences in aptitude were regarded as the result of unequal environmental pressures, not as due to hereditary equipment: 'The Marxist believes that human nature is not basically pre-ordained, but rests in the hands of man himself,'[4] and the whole notion of intelligence as innate ability became highly suspect. The influence of the Enlightenment is patent here, too. If Marx and Lenin were not, basically, egalitarian, it has to be admitted that there were initially strong egalitarian implications in the ideology of the system which they helped to evolve.

The notion of similarity of *outcome* has, of course, had its advocates in this country too. Thus Professor A.H. Halsey, after enunciating the principles of a 'New Socialist philosophy in the making', informs us that 'Social policy must treat unequal distributions, whether they originate in social inheritance or *genetic endowment*, as arbitrary. *Moreover, wealth and wit must be treated as social, not individual assets*' (my italics). Concerning the question 'What kinds of inequality can be regarded as legitimate?', he finds the 'most interesting ramification' of discussion 'in current debates concerning the displacement of the older liberal conception of equality of opportunity (in the sense of access) by the socialist notion of equality of outcome (in the sense of equal average attainment between non-educationally defined social groups).'[5] Such a philosophy 'justifies, *inter alia*, positive discrimination policies in education.' Professor Halsey fails to spell out the full implications of this 'socialist notion' – the one example he gives is drawn from racial or ethnic groups. It is, therefore, difficult to know how he would define his 'non-educationally defined social group' whose 'equal average educational attainments' must be secured. It is perhaps refreshing to discover that even Professor Halsey does not consider that every single child can be brought to the same level of attainment; but it requires only a little imagination to guess at the implications of his remarks for, say, middle-class vis-à-vis lower-working-class social groups in his search for 'equal average educational attainment' as between the two. Persistently and consistently the former perform better than the latter on average. Totalitarian methods of the most draconian kind (involving both positive and *negative* discriminations) would be required to equalise the average attainments of the two groups.

III

There is a further issue arising out of the intellectual and political events of the late eighteenth and early nineteenth centuries which is also of importance to our theme – the problem of cultural authority. As political authority was gradually extended to the masses the question of the maintenance of cultural standards implicit in the old aristocratic culture became increasingly pressing. J.S. Mill and Arnold, among others, both attempted to face this problem – and clearly, for education, it becomes one of central importance, though institutional inertia common to the development of societies has not made it a pressing one at school level until our own day. Nevertheless, the ideological issues implicit in the problem were argued throughout the nineteenth century. They were raised by the Utilitarian programme of reform and its appeal to the numerical majority as the true arbiters of moral and cultural purposes. Bentham's ethical theories rejected in any form the notion of an absolute hierarchy of values. A combination of utility and association psychology made man 'totally the product of circumstances and motivated solely by egoism'. Here was no principle of authority which could be appealed to to maintain a cultural tradition against temporary ebullitions of interest or desire.

Various attempts to face the dilemma implicit in the felt need for social reform and the equally pressing need to preserve a cultural heritage and the authority implicit in it were noted and have been excellently expounded by Dr Sheldon Rothblatt in his book *The Revolution of the Dons*. There Dr Rothblatt applies his analysis to the crisis over university education (expressly with reference to Cambridge) in the mid-nineteenth century. Mill sought a solution through the dissemination of educated men throughout the main institutions of Victorian society so that the principle of cultural authority would be diffused through the community at large. Arnold appealed to the state as the repository of cultural authority – culture being 'The best that has been thought and said.' Neither solution, of course, was satisfactory. It is necessary, however, to refer here briefly to the dilemma which Mill and Arnold – among many others – faced and which has been charted in detail by Professor Raymond Williams in *Culture and Society* (1780-1950) because the argument implies a third line of cultural and social concern relevant to my theme, in addition to the meritocratic and egalitarian strands indicated in the previous section — and one, moreover, in some degree of conflict with the other two. The implications of this third element I will reveal when I come to deal with the contribution of T.S. Eliot to the current debate over equality. For the moment, however, I wish to pursue further the implications of the other two.

IV

As we have already glimpsed, there are strong pressures towards equality *of outcome* in the work of John Dewey, the American educationist whose work raises questions of meaning and communication which take us to the central curricular issues of equality (conceived of as sameness) where education is concerned. To Dewey education is explicitly an instrument in the promotion of a more democratic society. The egalitarian implications of 'democracy' for him can be guessed at in his formulation of the characteristic features which he wishes to promote in his democratic society: 'A democracy is more than a form of government; it is primarily a mode of associated living, of conjoint communicated experience.'[6]

The emphasis is on the nature of the community experience. Democracy is more than a political device; the essence of the democratic way of life would seem to lie in the extension and proliferation of shared meanings ('interests') in contradistinction to those barriers of class, race or national territory which at present tend to prevent people from sharing a common experience. Dewey is too aware of the diversity of human make-up to count as a rigid egalitarian; nevertheless, there are strong equalising tendencies in the direction of sameness implicit in his views of men's developmental potential and in his asserted need for an increased community of experience open to all. He is a relentless enemy of the Platonic hierarchy: 'progress in knowledge has made us aware of the superficiality of Plato's lumping of individuals and their original powers into a few sharply marked-off classes; it has taught us that original capacities are indefinitely numerous and variable.'[7] At the same time he argues that a man would not be 'an individual if there was not something incommensurable about him.' Yet in the context the stress on 'incommensurability' is a strategy directed against the suggestion that men differ in levels of ability rather than a device for indicating an ultimate incommensurability between human beings. The argument is that men's talents are more varied than the hierarchy of class, with its implications of the sharp demarcation of human talents, would suggest. But the possible deduction that greater variety might make

115

communication even more difficult is avoided. In any case, the idea that some division into classes may be a rudimentary recognition of the variability of human endowment and provide an elementary way of coping with it in socially organisational terms does not, of course, strike Dewey.

Dewey's view of social efficiency, indeed, involves what he calls the 'socialization of mind': this necessitates 'breaking down the barriers of social stratification which make individuals impervious to the interests of others.' He desires a 'cultivated imagination for what men have in common and a rebellion at whatever unnecessarily divides them.' And, however much he may protest in the name of 'diversity' and 'incommensurability' it is difficult not to detect a strongly collectivist-egalitarian implication in his explicit repudiation of the cultivation of an 'inner' life as a desirable educational aim:[8]

> the idea of perfecting an 'inner' personality is a sure sign of social divisions. What is called inner is simply that which does not connect with others — which is not capable of free and full communication. What is termed spiritual culture has usually been futile, with something rotten about it, just because it has been conceived as a thing which a man might have internally — and therefore exclusively. What one is as a person is what one is as associated with others, in a free give and take of intercourse.

In the last sentence individuation seems to become co-extensive with socialisation: the person is dissolved into his social relationships.

The position, then, seems to be: everyone is unique and should have an opportunity of developing his 'distinctive' capacities; but what is developed should be equally capable of being communicated in its fullness to all, otherwise that social efficiency which results from the socialisation of mind will not be gained. It is interesting that in his view of desirable culture Dewey finds that all worthwhile accomplishments, manifestations of experience inherently praiseworthy, should be accompanied by results of value to others. The ideals of self-sacrifice and of self-perfection, both of which imply a self which exists apart from others, are not to be recommended, for they are both manifestations of a dualism which is inherently undesirable: 'for that reason, it is the particular task of education at the present time to struggle on behalf of an aim in which social efficiency and personal culture are synonyms instead of antagonists.'[9] Social efficiency, as we have seen, he equates with a widening of social sympathy, the socialisation of mind which leads to the breaking down of the barriers of social stratification. Hence the desired culture is manifest in 'the capacity for constantly expanding the range and accuracy of one's perception of meanings' in order to achieve the goal of complete cultural homogenisation: 'to have the same ideas about things which others have to be like-minded with them, and thus to be really members of a social group, is to attach the same meanings to things and to acts which others attach.'

This problem of meaning, as I have been hinting all along, is a crucial one for the egalitarian. One feature of Dewey's work may have helped to conceal this from him, another may indicate that indirectly he may have realised it. Dewey's major interest was in science, and his general philosophy amounted to an attempt to apply rather primitive scientific principles to life itself. Basically his instrumentalism involved the application of the technician's approach to everyday problems: to quote his own words, the 'hypothesis that works is the true one.' Now science provides meanings that are unequivocal; whether stated in words or formulae they should be capable of only one interpretation; nuance or ambiguity are rigorously excluded as of intent. Clearly, in the logical progression which makes up a science as a body of knowledge an individual student may reach a ceiling of understanding, but at least he is not faced with the complexities of ambiguity as an essential element in the very nature of the discourse he is studying. The early stages of a science are simple and wholly apparent; the poems of William Blake are simple but incredibly opaque. Difficulties over meaning may arise as a science advances because of increasing complexity and the gradual realisation that concepts *intended* to be unequivocal in meaning are, as a matter of fact, more ambiguous than suspected — but they are not built in to the very substance of the discourse. Behind the attempt at cultural homogenisation lies a shift in cultural attention, as science, rather than the arts, has constituted the paradigm of cultural meaning.[10] For when science is the paradigm of knowledge, there is likely to be a built-in prejudice in favour of finding meaning clear and communicable, especially if the science believed in is of a pretty elementary sort; and Dewey was still Baconian in his scientific outlook. When such a person comes to look at the arts (implying the traditional, 'aristocratic' arts springing out of the Renaissance tradition) he is likely to interpret them also as being equally open and clear to the gaze, and this is precisely what we find in Dewey: 'Since art is the most universal form of language, since it is constituted, even apart from literature, by the common qualities of the public world, it is the most universal and freest form of communication.'[11] Though he does see art as imaginative and innovative, he sees the experience of art as essentially shaped by traditional social experience and its expression as 'public and communicating' and as striking 'below the barriers that separate human beings from one another.' Mind, to Dewey, is a mode of activity, not an isolated entity within which things happen; it is therefore essentially in contact with its surroundings, 'objects and events, past, present and future'. It is little wonder, then, that he attended to the process of communication

117

rather than to the nature of what was being communicated by a mind necessarily separate from its fellows. Once you focus on the meaning of what is being communicated as a separate entity, you raise questions about its communicability and intelligibility as a received entity in another mind — and it is a short step from there to ask questions about the capacity of the receiving mind to receive. The notion of mind as an essentially public communicating organ focuses on the process rather than on the nature of what is communicated — hence the belief that 'barriers' to communication are removable by external social policies rather than built in to the very uniqueness of individual mind.

For to every message there must be a receptor; and meaning is the product of two separate acts of attention and will, not of a single process of interaction. Once seen in this way, the possibility of non-comprehension is apparent. What goes on *in* the mind of the communicator and what goes on *in* the mind of the recipient may be two different things. (One is forced to this metaphoric mode of expression, however painful to certain modern philosophers, by the need to identify two separate consciousnesses.) The communication of meanings is the basic function of education, and the crucial task which faces the educator is that of making his meaning clear and apparent. But failure to transmit is a universal experience of educationists and one of the fundamental reasons for this failure must, on occasions at least, be accorded to the sheer inability of the recipient to grasp what is offered — either because it is too 'difficult' or because by nature it is opaque and ambiguous in transmission. One is faced by a sheer dissimilarity of mental functioning, for whatever reason, a dissimilarity which, in part, can be defined in terms of various levels beyond which certain minds demonstrably do not grasp. I am not for the moment concerned with whether this inability stems from inherently inferior mental powers — the product of heredity — or whether it stems from unhappy experiences, for instance of an emotional nature, which produce emotional disturbances inimical to response. What I am concerned with is the gap which exists and can be shown by tests to exist, between the higher and subtler forms of meaning and what demonstrably certain pupils can grasp. The life of the educator is constantly brought to recognise the empirical validity of William Blake's famous aphorism that 'a fool sees not the same tree that a wise man sees.'

V

Now Dewey, in other parts of his work, seems implicitly to accept differentiations of level of response; for in his handling of the whole complex of meanings relevant to the life of an educational institution which we call a curriculum he seems to accept a priority of meanings in terms of those which have significance for the majority. The curriculum, he urges, must be organised in order to lay fundamental emphasis on the widest range of available meanings; everything else is to be regarded as frills: 'the curriculum must be planned with reference to placing essentials first and refinements second. The things which are socially most fundamental, that is, which have to do with the experiences in which the widest groups share, are the essentials.'[12] Here there is suggested an order of value priority which seems to imply that certain disciplines are beyond the range of certain people, indeed, of the majority itself — these constitute the 'refinements'. At the same time, such attribution of priority to some disciplines rather than to others is at odds with another statement where he repudiates any idea of a hierarchy of studies. Dewey does not deny that in certain circumstances it may be more desirable to follow one activity rather than another, but 'In the abstract or at large, apart from the needs of a particular situation in which choice has to be made, there is no such thing as degrees or order of value.'[13] One is, then, presented with a democracy of curricular objectives, each having its own intrinsic merit, and subject in choice apparently only to the momentary desire of the protagonist. Here there would seem to be an extended liberality. No criteria of relevant value other than the vague appeals to 'enrichment of life' and 'uniqueness' are allowed — and who could deny that in certain limited circumstances and in certain limited ways, even pushpin might be said to enrich life? A slackness of individual aspiration is encouraged — why bother when almost anything can gain approval? At the same time, in another context, a principle of choice is introduced in the idea of the prior importance of those curricular elements which have the widest appeal. The effect is to weaken resolve to tackle the difficult and the unpopular and to substitute the appeal of the universally acceptable if inevitably undemanding.

This shift of emphasis has a number of counterparts in the modern world. For instance, we are at present witnessing in our society an attack on traditional moral valuations — in the spheres of sex, authority and the like — which paradoxically seems to enhance the choice of the individual by making him/her the arbiter of how to behave, about whom to sleep with, whether to take drugs and so on. In other words there seems to be no principle of moral or cultural authority to which the individual can appeal other than personal whim and 'doing one's own thing'. At precisely the same time, certain other sorts of choices are being imposed — as to the sort of school to which one can send one's child for instance — in the name of social and public good. What we are seeing indeed is not so much a loosening of moral imperatives, but a shift of their nature and in the basis on which they are considered acceptable. What may be said to contribute to certain private moral aspirations and restraints is being broken down because these may perhaps reveal different qualities as between people, between those capable of self-discipline, for instance, and the self-indulgent. In the field of private morals, then, people are being encouraged to consider their whims and desires as ultimate criteria. In the public realm, however, a specific set of moral imperatives operate which are again directed against possible differentiations of life quality arising out of attendance at different educational institutions offering different curricular and therefore different life experiences. In both cases the net result is to foster a uniformity of life-style at a lower level of aspiration, in the one case by encouraging restriction of choice in a democracy of moral alternatives, there being no suggested principle of discrimination other than that of desire or want, and in the other by explicitly introducing, for example, 'commonness' ('the common school') as the sole offering. In the same way Dewey proclaims that each school subject has an intrinsic worth and deprives the seeker of principles in terms of which he may judge the relative value of what he is offered — and at the same time offers as the exclusive principle of choice the social criterion of majority capacity.

The aim, then, would seem to be to destroy 'aristocratic' differentiation and substitute, as the principle of cultural authority, majority cultural experience: Dewey here is symptomatic of what later was to appear in this country. Hence the attacks on the public schools, the grammar schools and even the universities in the name of comprehensivisation; hence the insistence on the common curriculum in the comprehensive schools for the first two or three years and the imputed need for all to gain a common social experience under the same roof. Of course, it will not work, because it encounters an essential and irreducible hierarchy implicit in the structures of meaning which make up the school curriculum. It is possible to slough off certain traditional elements redolent of an inegalitarian past, such as Latin and Greek. But it is not possible to democratise the curriculum beyond a certain point simply because some at least of the traditional meaning-structures — in the sciences and technology, for instance, which are only superficially democratic even if 'open' and in theory inspectable by all — are essential as ways of implementing the running of the modern world. Put it another way, one is faced, at last, with the ineluctable necessity of selecting certain sorts of expertise, people who have grasped advanced technical or scientific principles necessary for keeping the machines running. Paradoxically, what started as democratic and, within limits, egalitarian (i.e. science), has achieved a logical complexity which demands high expertise and high intelligence, of a sort, for its full understanding. The arts can be, are to some extent being, democratised and proletarianised, as indeed they have become in the post-Dada period, especially our own period of the counter- or anti-culture. For Dada represented a demotic snook-cocking at the whole essentially aristocratic Renaissance tradition — and the reverberations of Dada have spread far into the modern art movement, in the conscious break with tradition, the emphasis on momentary impulse or skeletal abstraction, in the very abdication of the artist himself and the appeal of chance. The hierarchical principle — in the form of meritocracy — has passed, for the time, paradoxically, to the sciences. And modern science does not support Dewey's essentially primitive view of its universal communicability.[14]

Dewey, then, represents in the American environment a foretaste of the attack on that value differentiation in meaning which sustained the aristocratic principle throughout the centuries. He points forward to a developing situation which we face in the 1980s. Egalitarianism has passed beyond the phase of seeking to establish certain equalities of a specific nature — before the law for instance, or in the right to vote; it is attempting to invade the very spheres of cultural 'experience' itself.[15] This is one of the reasons why Dewey is so symptomatic a figure: in him we find a view of experience, of meaning, which increasingly is invading the central areas of our culture — though in ways which it is reasonable to suppose Dewey himself would never have guessed. He might indeed have been repelled by much of what today he would see.

VI

Of course, there have been reassertions of the Renaissance principle in the sphere of the humanities. In his opposition to both the egalitarian and the meritocratic we see the significance of the contribution of T.S. Eliot both to our thinking about our culture and to education as a manifestation of that culture. Eliot, in an oblique way, takes up the theme of cultural authority mooted in section III — 'oblique' because he did not attempt to face the problem which exercised Mill and others as to how we were to justify the value differentiation implicit in the old aristocratic culture, but rather set about the sociological task of defining the conditions under which the traditional culture could flourish given the assumption that we wished to preserve it. In the process of doing so he introduces a factor of equality absent from many nineteenth-century discussions of the problem, which were broadly concerned with locating the principles on which a high minority culture could be preserved and justified. Eliot's innovation is to see the problem of high culture as only *part* of the problem of preserving a healthy state of culture. To achieve such preservation it is certainly necessary to

121

preserve the quality of the culture of the minority by keeping it a minority culture; but in addition, *every* level in the community needs to contribute its appropriate cultural offering, at the level of consciousness it can achieve, in order that the well-being of the whole shall be preserved. After all, 'Fine arts is the refinement, not the antithesis of popular art'; the minority, Eliot thinks, cannot sustain itself in isolation, cut off from society at large and the nourishment a healthy popular art can provide. In Eliot's view, then, each level of the community must make a contribution which is *equally* appropriate but necessarily different.

In his attempt to define the sociological conditions in terms of which each section of the population can make this appropriate contribution, Eliot departs from the atomisation of individual offering implicit in both the egalitarian and the meritocratic view of educational opportunity. The assumption throughout his work is that people are not capable of achieving similar levels of consciousness and attempts to equalise even opportunity may produce unfortunate results. He once said: 'You can have equality; you can have culture; but you cannot have both.'[16] The 'headlong rush to educate everyone' (i.e. to afford everyone opportunities) was, he considered, leading to a lowering of standards. Why should this be so?

Eliot's answer to this crucial question can be inferred from his cultural diagnosis, where indeed it is all but explicitly stated. As we have seen, he clearly accepted as empirical fact the manifestation of different levels of consciousness among the individuals of the community: but he saw that such different levels of consciousness arose from more than simply individual differences in measured capacity. He noted that the primary agency for the transmission of our culture was not, as the modern world sees it, the individual as an atomic entity but the family as manifest in the lives of different generations of that family. Environmentalists challenge the view that such differences in achievement as undoubtedly exist are inevitable; they tend to put them down to the force of unpropitious external circumstances, bad housing or schooling, but they confine the argument within the limits of the negative effects of these factors on the releasing of talent. To some extent Eliot accepts the environmentalist case but urges that the intimacies of family cultural continuity afford a positive case for differentiating those capable of high levels of consciousness from the rest. In other words, he advises that we should be more aware of the *positive* advantages to the health of our culture in having certain persisting families at the highest levels who can supplement the work of the formal system by the nature of their informal interests and commitments. Here both heredity and propitious environment can work positively to maintain the appropriate level of consciousness.

Let me expand this further. The communication problem lies at the heart of Eliot's social and specifically educational thinking. He sees education as one means of transmitting the culture from generation to generation. But he also sees that the formal education system can only transmit part of that culture:[17]

> There is . . . a danger of interpreting 'education' to cover both too much and too little; too little, when it implies that education is limited to what can be taught; too much, when it implies that everything worth preserving can be transmitted by teaching.

Hence, for instance, the need for a continuity of families charged with the transmission of the most conscious part of the culture. This, he states, does not constitute a 'defence of aristocracy', but a 'plea for a form of society in which an aristocracy should have a peculiar and essential function, as peculiar and essential as the function of any other part of society.' Put another way, he implied that in the consciousness of certain family environments there is an accumulation of cultural and social wisdom which, if neglected, can only lead to a general social deprivation. Meritocracy is not enough because meritocrats meet only in terms of a specific expertise, of a professional interest; thus 'they will meet like committees', and will communicate only at this level, at which much of the nuance and subtlety of cultural meaning will be lost. 'Men who meet only for definite serious purposes, and on official occasions, do not wholly meet.'[18] A society based on meritocracy implies a too great mobility and this in turn a lack of a continuity of meanings.

The great service which this analysis by Eliot performs is to draw attention to the respective roles of both formal and informal education. A system of education is essentially a formal structure, and teachers and pupils meet in terms of explicit and conscious learning structures. These structures, as a matter of fact, are primarily cognitive, in the very nature of the modern school curriculum. But one of the major themes of Eliot's poetry is that of the complexity of meaning and communication. In it he speaks of the 'intolerable wrestle with words and meanings'; but more, he is haunted by the power of memory and the indestructible quality of time: 'time future' is contained in 'time past'.[19] So consciousness is inevitably and unavoidably an historical consciousness with 'a lifetime burning in every moment',[20] not simply an individual one.

This sense of the historical dimension makes him aware that communication is of many different kinds, some of them much more subtle than can be made explicit in a classroom lesson. Furthermore, he stresses that the subtler sorts of communication take place through the informal agencies of our society:[21]

For the schools can transmit only a part, and they can only transmit this part effectively, if the outside influences, not only of family and environment, but of work and play, of newsprint and spectacles and entertainment and sport, are in harmony with them.

That informal agencies play a vital role in the whole business of cultural transmission is irrefutable. As Dr Rupert Wilkinson has pointed out in his book *The Prefects*, the informal elements in a public boarding school have tended to play the major socialising role in the upbringing of its inhabitants, rather than what is explicitly taught. The pressures (to use Wilkinson's terminology) are aesthetic and manifest in etiquette and 'good form'; the classical curriculum, the explicit subject-matter of 'teaching', though not entirely unproductive, has proved a narrower and less broadening affair than it has been made out to be because of the way it has been taught. The long hours of translation left little time, as Wilkinson points out, for the broader considerations of literary content and meaning. It was the profoundly influential *style* of the school life which produced the much more lasting effect – its emphasis on loyalty and co-operation, its acceptance of minute differentiations of rank, its dissolution of youthful egotism, the assumed association of social status with moral superiority, its reference back to a certain class of family life: what, in fact, is now known as the 'hidden curriculum'. In the same way, in other spheres we have become aware of the profound influence of the home environment, so that the efforts of schools are often brought to nought unless their work is backed up by parental support. This indeed has been so well documented as hardly to require elaboration; it remains a constant barrier to the self-realisation of certain working-class children who sometimes fall behind their middle-class peers not necessarily because of lack of ability but because of lack of parental support and because of cultural deprivation in the home. Dr J.W.B. Douglas's evidence in *The Home and the School* has been widely accepted in its view of the profound influence the home has on educational success. But if families have this negative effect they may also be allowed to have a positive effect, though this is not the inference which has so commonly been drawn from the findings. If subtle matters of attitudes among parents produce this considerable effect on the learning characteristics of their offspring, is not the whole question of indirect informal educative influence of the profoundest importance, and is it not likely also to affect those subtleties of meaning and communication with which Eliot is concerned?

Now as a matter of undeniable empirical fact we are faced, in the schools, for whatever reason – be it heredity or environment – with a vast differentiation in terms of levels of measured achievement. This is the primary datum of the educational situation. Some interpretations of the notion of social justice would seem to indicate an attempt at equalisation of achievement by a vast programme of compensatory education, on the grounds that present deficiencies spring largely from environmental shortcomings. What, however, no one could possibly contemplate is an attempt to equalise parents in terms of cultural commitment. Yet some such enterprise would seem essential if compensatory education is to have any real chance of producing lasting results. In other words, it is necessary, assuming the accepted importance of informal education, to compensate not only within the formal system, but within the informal system also. Once stated in this way, the difficulty of the notion of compensatory education and the reason for its comparative lack of success in America become more apparent.

There are, indeed, two possible interpretations of the idea of social justice. Normally it is interpreted in terms of an equalisation of provision for the individual members of society, who are regarded as having prior claim to attention. In this sense, the notion has become either a device of the meritocracy to ensure the identification of talent or a means by which the egalitarian society seeks to induce a sameness of cultural experience. A more profound interpretation of the notion, however, might have regard to the benefit accruing to all from a revival of cultural vitality, i.e. 'justice' to the conditions necessary for cultural health rather than justice to atomic individuals in society. The difference lies in whether the individual or the state of society is accorded priority.

If we admit the claims of society in terms of its cultural health then we need to note carefully the historical pressures implicit in the society as a going cultural concern. Granted that historically the hierarchic order of society has never matched precisely the diffusion of cultural levels of consciousness throughout the community – which is why a degree of mobility has always been important – we may note nevertheless that some social continuity of such levels is implicit in the primary unit of all known historical societies, the family. Hence, paradoxically, even to do justice to individuals it becomes necessary not to impose a common curriculum on all irrespective of observed ability to benefit (to treat education as an 'abstraction', as Eliot puts it, according to which 'it has come to be assumed that there must be one measure of education according to which everyone is educated simply more or less')[22] but to seek curricular differentiation in ways which allow all an equal opportunity to achieve their appropriate level of consciousness and hence to make their own proper contribution to the cultural health of the society. In other words, we should look to the viability of the offering rather than seek to impose a uniformity, a sameness, where the living complexity of individuals within the social order makes this unacceptable.

Those concerned with a greater equalisation of opportunity for individuals have had their way for some time because, appalled by the spectacle of historical poverty, the desirability of some equalisation of shares (of what beyond economic resources has usually gone undefined with any distinctness) as a means to ameliorating the lot of the deprived has seemed of paramount importance. Though complete equality of income has not been achieved nor seriously contemplated, a greater equality of income and of access to remunerative positions, and the banishment of the problems of extreme poverty to the margins of our lives have been achieved. Some such equalisation in the economic sphere can be regarded as desirable; but the notion of more equal shares cannot so easily be transferred to other spheres. Differentiation of job remuneration can be compensated for by artificial devices of the economy; differentiation of minds imposes irreducible limits to attempts to induce a sameness of cultural experience, more especially when 'mind' is seen to be a matter of interaction between hereditary endowment and early cultural opportunity.

The position where education is concerned is complicated because the educational system fulfils two separate functions. One is that of cultural transmission where it is sensible to seek to transmit that level of culture which the pupil can encompass; the other provides the means by which the occupational system is fed. The desire, therefore, to afford people, economically, equal chances interferes with the more basic need to induct people into that level of culture from which they may gain most satisfaction. If the aim is simply to recruit to the meritocracy, then similarity of provision becomes excusable on the grounds that all should as long as possible be in a position to achieve the desired occupational goals; the prices to be paid are unsuitability of provision for many who demonstrably fail to benefit — and to some extent the distortion of what is provided by the need to prepare candidates to leap the necessary hurdles. The seeking of cultural satisfaction — the aim of the liberal educationist throughout the ages — is in some degree of tension with the need to provide life chances. This has been recognised from the time of Aristotle onwards — it has always been emphasised that a liberal education is intended for leisure; and, today, a liberal education exists in a particular state of tension with that demand for expertise which is so much the aim of modern specialised education.

In an age which has learnt to accept (almost) the priority of the economy above all things, it makes sense to ask if the culture matters. When the answer is that it is the culture which structures the highest and most complex human consciousness of the age and that the economy constitutes simply one aspect of that culture, it is perhaps not too much to claim that it does. Culture, of course, is a word that can be used in both a neutral (in the sense of the total pattern of a

126

society's thought and doings), and an evaluative sense, as (to quote Matthew Arnold again) the 'best that has been thought and said.' Education is a concept that carries with it inevitably evaluative overtones, and it is culture in its evaluative sense which is relevant to its functioning. In other words, the culture the school is concerned to transmit constitutes, basically, the truth-meanings of its generation. It is therefore surely fundamental to the quality of the life of its times, and individuals will be the richer for submitting themselves to the requirements of a vital cultural order rather than claiming consideration solely as atomic economic units.

VII

It is desirable briefly to recapitulate the characteristics of the three main positions which have emerged from my analysis of the historical movement towards equality which has culminated in our own day. I will distinguish these as the egalitarian, the meritocratic and the cultural, and I will attempt to spell out some of their implications in purely educational terms.

The egalitarian seeks to achieve the maximum sameness possible, a sameness which, at secondary level, should not only become manifest in the provision of a common school which all should attend, but in a subjection to similarity of curricular requirement, even, indeed, to quote the LCC's pamphlet 'London Comprehensive Schools', 'to have, as far as possible, a common syllabus'. The egalitarian's fundamental aim is a common social experience, as many and as varied points of common social contact, to quote Dewey. His aim is the common cultural meaning, his instruments compensatory education, the common school, the common curriculum and the internal organisation of non-streaming among others.

The meritocrat will be concerned with sameness at the beginning of secondary schooling because of the difficulties of selection and the social need to identify talent. He will want a common curriculum not in order to provide a common social experience but in order to hold open the options of selection as long as possible; without some common element in what is learnt, transfer between streams, for instance, becomes difficult. In general, however, he will approve of internal setting and/or streaming, and the teaching of the ablest children by the most highly qualified teachers. The tendency here will be for hierarchic tripartitism to reproduce itself inside the comprehensive school. His fundamental purposes, however, will be examination success and the close relevance of school provision to occupational requirement.

In both these positions the aim is ultimately social-functional. The

127

egalitarian desires social harmony through the abolition of barriers dividing man from man, seeking in the last resort the equalisation of meaning as between mind and mind, so that all come to *mean* the same thing in a heavenly bliss of classlessness and harmony of interests and purposes. The meritocrat is not so naive. He sees that the actual functioning of the society for which he is seeking to educate makes certain irreducible demands — for instance, in terms of specific expertise of a scientific and technological nature. As the functioning of society is essentially hierarchical and not all can occupy the top governmental or expert positions — nor are all capable of doing so — his educational aims are tied to the occupational structure, so that society is fed with the varieties of expertise it needs for its efficient functioning: functional efficiency, the production of 'educated manpower', sums up his aspirations.

The cultural position is different. Here there will be a tendency to accept the diversity of talent with which we are faced as giving some indication of the different levels of cultural consciousness for which he should provide. Anyone who holds the cultural position will, indeed, be hostile to any attempts at equalisation of meaning except in the fundamental sense that each pupil should be provided with an education which, although showing great diversity and difference in content, nevertheless attempts to be equally appropriate to his or her level of potential. His scepticism over any equalising in the content of provision will spring partly from his acceptance of the importance of the hereditary and early environmental elements in assessing the possible ceilings of human attainment — though he will concede that wise educational provision may exploit successfully an inevitable imbalance in the generations which allows a certain measure of flexibility for the possible development of talent. He will, however, consider that this can be more easily achieved by special and varied provision exploiting what is known about the various ability levels than through an attempt to impose a common though unsuitable provision and thus evoking repugnance among sections of the school population. For he is impressed by the fact that human beings are more difficult to engineer than the physical environment and that the individual pupil is subject to pressures which lie deep in the historical consciousness of the race. Such a pupil should not, therefore, be treated as an atomic unit apart from family culture and the psychic expectations implicit in family culture. These indeed will work both ways, at once assisting the school experience of certain sections and tending to make the school an alien institution to those whose life and family experience foster different priorities — though there will, of course, be exceptions to these. He therefore will seek to encourage that level of cultural commitment which is feasible in the light of a careful sociocultural analysis which includes an historical as well as purely individual dimension — though he will bear in mind T.S. Eliot's warning, when speaking of a 'continuous gradation of cultural levels', 'it is important to remember that we should not consider the upper levels as possessing *more* culture than the lower, but as representing a more conscious culture and a greater specialisation of culture.'[23] His aim, indeed, will be liberal rather than functional, his concern with quality and inherent satisfaction rather than status as such. What, indeed, is claimed for him is that, his analysis of the human predicament being the more profound, what he has to offer shames the thinner rationalism implicit in the diagnoses of the other two. Cultural diversity and the satisfaction that appropriate cultural offerings can foster provide a richer quality of living than either harmonisation of interests based on a reduction of all human wants and achievements to the same level, or the limitation of differentiation to functional provision.

VIII

It will be appreciated that it is rare to find any of the three positions outlined above in their purest forms. Perhaps it should also be noted that it is rare to find the last of the three at all.

The implementation of comprehensive education has predictably revealed the incompatibility of the meritocratic and the egalitarian models, both of which in many such schools have had their supporters. The resultant tensions within institutions between those who are committed to greater equality of opportunity so that more may be afforded an opportunity of becoming unequal, and those who look to greater equality of outcome (structurally manifest in mixed-ability teaching and indiscriminate staff allocation, so that able children are not assigned to the academically most competent teachers) have contributed to that mediocritisation which, in too many comprehensives, is the unmistakable outcome. The government's assisted places scheme is merely the overt and concrete manifestation of widespread fears lest able children be denied their opportunities, especially those from neighbourhood comprehensives in poor areas. No one can seriously think that a hard-up government would willingly dispense these millions unless there was convincing evidence of deprivation.

Yet at a time when the relative failure of comprehensive schooling as a blanket solution to our difficulties over selection is becoming apparent to all,[24] a Conservative Government, while rightly providing a bolt-hole for the able, continues to press the claims of a considerable area of curricular homogeneity for the rest. We are thus faced with such monstrosities as children, hardly able to read or write their own language, having to learn a foreign one as well. One of the most important and pressing needs in education in this country today is to develop a theory of popular education which will provide genuine opportunities for those who figure in the Schools Council enquiry *Young School Leavers* as the bored, frustrated and rebellious − the less intelligent from the culturally restricted home.

IX

It is here indeed that the relevance of the cultural model I have developed earlier is perhaps most easily apparent in the circumstances of today. The attempt at cultural homogenisation explicit in the meanings of the watered-down, high-cultural curriculum which is their traditional school fodder has lamentably and palpably failed. Yet we lack a theory of popular education which would provide the children I refer to with *cultural* satisfactions designed to afford them the opportunity to live rewarding lives. They are drop-outs of the meritocratic system; they are the victims of an inability to grasp the meanings implicit in the well-intentioned egalitarian attempt to provide a common experience.

The aim must be to provide them with an education which, while admitting their incapacity for certain types of advanced cognitive education, nevertheless genuinely liberalises. Work has, for such children, become too narrow and restricted in scope in the modern factory to provide, as traditionally it did, a focal point for the extension of their awareness of significant meaning. Nor must they be dismissed with a simple life-adjustment programme which seeks to exploit everyday practicability at the most mundane levels − counting the change and mending the motor bike.

I have written at greater length elsewhere about this revised syllabus and its rationale in terms of their level of consciousness in my *Dilemmas of the Curriculum*. What is interesting, as I there point out, is that certain radical educators have appreciated the unsuitability of the common curriculum for children, for instance, from a working-class 'culture' − and indeed make their own suggestions of alternative curricula. In the book mentioned, I analyse the qualitative inadequacies of these suggestions. What, however, remains significant is that the unsuitability of the common offering is becoming more widely appreciated and that I am no longer a lone voice suggesting differentiation.

My purpose in this brief reference is simply to bring out the relevance and applicability of the cultural model in preference to either the meritocratic or the egalitarian views I have analysed. For at bottom both these imply a false notion of equality, though more so in the latter than in the former case. The fault of the meritocratic model lies in its too frequent indifference to the living potential by which we are faced in order to serve the purely functional efficiency of the industrial-bureaucratic society. That some concessions in this direction are necessary, indeed inevitable, is no justification for not considering the price we pay for not working out an adequate theory of education for the less able. Yet in the meritocratic school at least certain sections of the potential are reasonably catered for. The able are not neglected or despised. The fault of the egalitarian model lies even deeper – a perverse attempt to homogenise both ends of the spectrum in a mediocre common experience satisfying to neither. The attempt to induce a common meaning constitutes a most serious threat to the future of our civilisation – it degrades the able without satisfying the intellectually backward. The cultural model at least looks to satisfactions beyond the functional, and to an attempt to provide an equally appropriate but essentially differentiated school experience – differentiated in terms of cultural expectation and potential. Educationally this is the only sort of equality which is viable, for the abstract 'sameness' which produces the political solution of 'one man, one vote' is simply not possible within the complex requirements of a curriculum. Here, the very nature of the meanings concerned, their specifically involved and complex structures, palpably and unmistakably fail to coalesce with minds too restricted in capacity for cognitive development to benefit. The hope that such restrictions are the result of environmental pressures (and thus, it is thought, subject to manipulation) rather than hereditary endowment has recently taken so many knocks (notably from Professors Eysenck, Jensen and Butcher, among others) that it can be dismissed.[25] Ineluctably we are faced with a broad spectrum of talent, and its need for diversified cultural satisfactions appropriate to its varied levels of consciousness. In this way, we could aspire to a revitalised cultural order and the *individual* satisfactions this could afford – a forlorn hope, perhaps, in the degradation of our times, but worth the consideration of good men.

One strategy certainly we must avoid – the introduction of 'pop' culture into schools, on the grounds that this has become the new 'folk' culture and is therefore 'relevant'. This strategy is accompanied and sustained by all sorts of pretentious claims for 'pop', especially in the field of music. (The mingling of 'high' and 'pop' elements by the avant-garde is a matter of great social interest and cause for some concern.) Pop is largely about profits – as *Vox Pop* by Michael Wale, a book in no way hostile to pop, makes clear. At its best it provides distraction, as did the popular music of the 1920s and 1930s, to which it is no whit superior; indeed, it is appreciably worse mannered. Its introduction into schools should be strongly resisted. We have yet to count the cost of the comprehensive school, not only in terms of lost opportunities by individual children but also in subtler cultural matters. For as the attempt to meet the problem of heterogeneity in a homogeneous way develops, the temptation to provide what is culturally the lowest common denomination will grow. Yet however it may serve the hours of distraction, to bring it into school degrades the very notion of education as an initiation into excellence *at all levels*. Less emphasis on the contemporary (which too often assimilates pop and high culture in a mish-mash of mediocrity) and more on the accumulated riches (folk and high) of our historical culture is essential. Certainly it would afford a possible approach to that dilemma which has exercised the minds of some of the foremost thinkers of the last two centuries — the dilemma posed by the appreciation of the need to ameliorate the lot of the oppressed majority and at the same time preserve something of that quality of European culture which had depended on an aristocratic leisure and patronage. Furthermore, it would enable us to avoid yet another manifestation of the 'parochialism of the present'.

Notes

Introduction

1 'The depreciation of historical fact is deeply, and probably functionally, engrained in the ideology of the scientific profession' (T.S. Kuhn, *The Structure of Scientific Revolutions*, 2nd edn, University of Chicago Press, International Encyclopedia of Unified Sciences, 1970).
2 I refer especially to the work of Professor Bernstein: whatever criticism it may have evoked (and it seems to have stimulated a minor industry) it is marked by a penetrating insight into the role of language in the classroom and subtleties of usage which raise vitally important questions for teachers.
3 Cf. P. Bourdieu and J.C. Passeron, *Reproduction in Education, Society and Culture*, trans. R. Nice, Sage Publications, London, 1977. This is not to suggest that I necessarily endorse the findings; I merely note the subtlety of the analysis within its terms of reference.

Chapter 1 The parochialism of the present: some reflections on the history of educational theory

1 Cf. P.H. Hirst, 'Educational Theory', in J.W. Tibble (ed.), *The Study of Education*, London, Routledge & Kegan Paul, 1966, pp. 29-58.
2 Cf. W.J. Ong, *Rhetoric, Romance, and Technology*, Cornell University Press, 1971; especially the first four chapters.
3 Cf. E. Durkheim, *The Evolution of Educational Thought*; trans. P. Collins, London, Routledge & Kegan Paul, 1977, pp. 215-16.
4 W.H. Woodward, *Vittorino da Feltre and Other Humanist Educators*, Teachers' College, Columbia University, 1963, p. 105.
5 Cf. W.H. Woodward, *Desiderius Erasmus Concerning the Aim and Method of Education*, Teachers College, Columbia University,

1964, p. 128.

6 Cf. J.M. Lechner, *Renaissance Concepts of the Commonplaces*, New York, Pageant Press, 1962, passim.

7 This is important. Erasmus wrote a dialogue *Ciceronianus* (1528) in which he ridiculed the slavish follower of Cicero and appealed for a classically pure Latin which nevertheless was adapted to *original* work. Cf. Woodward, *Erasmus* op. cit., pp. 171, 200. Briefly, at its best, the humanist ideal of 'imitation' involved the internalisation of the best models and their redeployment in personal utterance; even then, however, the reliance on classical style and experience was heavy. Erasmus stresses the pedagogic importance of memory.

8 M. Baxandall, *Giotto and the Orators*, Oxford University Press, 1971, p. 46.

9 Cf. Sister Miriam Joseph, *Shakespeare's Use of the Arts of Language*, Columbia University Press, 1949, p. 5.

10 Woodward, *Erasmus*, op. cit., p. 213.

11 Sub-titled *The Renaissance Man and his Roles*, Yale University Press, 1973.

12 Ibid., p. 67.

13 Rousseau, *Emile*, trans. B. Foxley, Everyman edition, London; J.M. Dent, 1943, p. 56.

14 Castiglione, *The Book of the Courtier*, trans. G. Bull, Harmondsworth, Penguin, 1967, p. 66.

15 Cf. Michael Levey, *High Renaissance*, Harmondsworth, Penguin, 1975, p. 20.

16 Benedetto Varchi, cf. Levey, op. cit., p. 38.

17 Francis Bacon in M.T. McClure, Bacon's *Selections*, New York, Scribner's, 1928, p. 66.

18 Ibid., p. 123.

19 Cf. S. Anglo, 'The Courtier', in A.G. Dickens (ed.), *The Courts of Europe*, London, Thames & Hudson, 1977, especially pp. 42-4.

20 The account that follows relies extensively on T.W. Baldwin, *William Shakspere's 'Smalle Latine & Lesse Greek'*, 2 vols, University of Illinois Press, 1944. This massive work of historical reconstruction gives a detailed picture of humanist education in grammar and especially rhetoric as it was to be found in the grammar schools of Shakespeare's times and then shows how Shakespeare must have assimilated this learning and deployed it in his plays. There is no actual record of Shakespeare's having attended the Stratford grammar school, but the circumstantial evidence of his having had a full grammar school education is so overwhelming as to be virtually unassailable. Cf. also Donald L. Clark, *John Milton at St. Paul's School*, Columbia University Press, 1948. The rhetorical nature of Elizabethan writing is, in general, well established and the number of literary figures produced by so small a country so relatively considerable that it is hardly unreasonable to extrapolate, from the well-documented case of Shakespeare, the successful and fruitful assimilation of the rhetorical training in many other cases

– the effect of which was to make the Elizabethans not only verbally adept in creation but also in consumption. Critics have for long drawn attention to the verbal dexterity of the Elizabethan audience.

21 Joseph, *Shakespeare's Use of the Arts of Language*, op. cit.

22 R.S. Peters, 'Reason and passion', in R.F. Dearden, P.H. Hirst and R.S. Peters (eds), *Education and the Development of Reason*, London, Routledge & Kegan Paul, 1972, p. 210.

23 Cf. Ian Watt, *The Rise of the Novel*, London, Chatto & Windus, 1957, chapter 1.

24 Cf. Leon Edel, *The Life of Henry James*, Harmondsworth, Penguin, 1977, vol. 1, pp. 620-1.

25 Ibid., p. 728.

26 G. Ryle, 'A rational animal' in R.F. Dearden, P.H. Hirst and R.S. Peters (eds), op. cit., p. 190. Cf. K. Popper, 'The wrong view of science betrays itself in the craving to be right.'

27 J. Passmore, 'On teaching to be critical', ibid., p. 420.

28 Cf. Locke's epistle to the reader of his *Essay Concerning Human Understanding*, Everyman edition, 1947, p. xxiii.

29 Cf. Henry James, 'The great thing is to be *saturated* with something – that is, in one way or another, with life.'

30 Cf. Antony Quinton, 'Authority and autonomy of knowledge', *Proceedings of the Philosophy of Education Society of Great Britain*, 5, July 1971, pp. 201-15.

31 Something of the same picture of the normal conventionality of scientific research emerges from Thomas Kuhn's, *The Structure of Scientific Revolutions*, University of Chicago Press, International Encyclopedia of Unified Science, vol. 2, no. 2. Paradigm change is much more the exception than the rule.

32 Cf. F. Gilot and C. Lake, *Life with Picasso*, Harmondsworth, Penguin, 1966.

33 F.R. Leavis (ed.), *Mill on Bentham and Coleridge*, London, Chatto & Windus, 1950, p. 58.

34 Ibid., p. 59.

35 Ibid., pp. 60-1.

36 R.S. Peters, 'Reason and passion' in R.F. Dearden, P.H. Hirst and R.S. Peters (eds), op. cit., p. 211.

37 In his review of my *Studies in the History of Educational Theory*, vol. 1, Professor K. Charlton writes in rebuke 'Deriving what are considered to be the realities of the present from the prescriptions of the past is a dangerous game' (*Times Higher Educational Supplement*, 31 October 1980). Of course, it *can* be a dangerous game, for human knowledge is imperfect and always liable to misinterpretation. Unhappily there is no alternative; our view of the reality of the present can only be arrived at on the basis of the past – of personal memory which we call 'experience' or of that extended memory that we refer to as 'history' and which we add to our 'experience' by study. For however much the study of the past

may reveal discontinuities, questions and answers which for a variety of reasons no longer remain living issues, it must always afford opportunities for insight into the great human perennial problems such as power or love, nurture or aggression, etc. Just as in drawing on one's own personal experience of the past, it is important not to misinterpret that experience in facing current dilemmas (as Anthony Eden, for instance, is said to have misinterpreted the problem of Suez by false analogy with the very different experiential circumstances of Hitler's Germany in which he was also involved) so in appealing to historical circumstances it is important to bear in mind and allow for the possibly changed circumstances of apparently analogous affairs. This is where the historical imagination comes in, the need to reassess the categories of one's thinking. But to urge that no lessons can be drawn from history would be to deny any role to memory in human affairs, which is clearly impossible. I believe that Collingwood was right in these propositions that he offered about historical study: 'that the past which an historian studies is not a dead past, but a past which in some sense is still living in the present.' 'The historian's business is to reveal the less obvious features hidden from a careless eye in the present situation. What history can bring to moral and political life is a trained eye for the situation in which one has to act' (R.G. Collingwood, *An Autobiography*, Oxford University Press, 1978, Chapter IX). Though Collingwood was very conscious that 'answers' (historical events) were very much bound up with 'questions' specific to the era in which they occurred, he still saw history as the 'science of human affairs', throwing light on the present and helping us in our moral choices. And rightly so; the very language we use is an historical phenomenon. A comprehensive dictionary is always an historical report. Some words come labelled 'archaic', others 'rare'. Some demonstrate subtle shifts of meaning over the centuries, some remain remarkably fixed and static. But few other than newly invented technical terms fail to reveal some sort of history. If then our very tools of discourse and communication themselves constitute historical artefacts, how can we avoid history in other respects? Even value judgments in our historical exposition become, in some degree, unavoidable, as Sir Isaiah Berlin has argued in the Introduction to his *Four Essays on Liberty* (Oxford University Press, 1977) 'Detachment is itself a moral position. The use of neutral language . . . conveys its own ethical tone' (p. xxix).

Chapter 2 Literature and the social sciences: with particular reference to the sociology of education

1 By social scientist in this paper, I imply primarily the sociologist and the social psychologist.
2 F.O. Mathiessen and K.B. Murdoch (eds), *The Notebooks of Henry*

James, New York, Oxford University Press, 1947, p. 79.

3   Ibid., p. 82.
4   Ibid., pp. 82-4. The incidents related, considerably modified, influenced James's writing of his short novel *The Reverberator.*
5   The original is reprinted in *The Use of English,* vol. 2, no. 4, Summer 1951.
6   Cf. *The Phenomenology of the Social World,* Northwestern University Press, 1967, pp. 86-96.
7   Indeed, even in face-to-face situations some degree of typification is necessary, for we can never know *all* about another.
8   *The Phenomenology of the Social World,* op. cit., p. 105.
9   Cf. ibid., pp. 181-207.
10 'Common-sense and scientific interpretation of human action' in *Philosophy and Phenomenological Research,* vol. 14, no. 1, September 1963, p. 28.
11 Ibid., p. 31.
12 'Concept and theory in the social sciences', *Collected Papers,* M. Matanson (ed.), The Hague, Martinus Nijhoff, 1967, vol. 1, pp. 63-4.
13 'Common-sense and scientific interpretation', op. cit., p. 35.
14 Cf. R. Liddell, *A Treatise on the Novel,* London, Jonathan Cape, 1947, p. 90.
15 Cf. 'The education of the emotions' in G.H. Bantock, *Education Culture and the Emotions,* London, Faber & Faber, 1967.
16 I am not, of course, suggesting that social scientists investigating the phenomena of murder would miss these implications. I simply wish to emphasise that *expression* matters and that different formulations imply, in some degree, different *meanings.* One of the great forms of precision of linguistic expression is literature.
17 Ronald King, *Values and Involvement in a Grammar School,* London, Routledge & Kegan Paul, 1969, pp. 63-4.
18 He may, of course, argue that values chosen from four authorities are more 'objective' than those chosen by one. As, however, in the last resort his is the final choice as to which value to put forward, as I have shown, this argument falls to the ground.
19 Frances Stevens, *The Living Tradition,* London, Hutchinson, 1960, pp. 94 and 95.
20 Extreme claims to scientific objectivity on the part of sociologists have, of course, been abandoned; sociology has 'largely abandoned the quest for universal generalisations that are always applicable to the class to which they refer. Sociologists are quite content to establish uniformities with a high probability of recurrence.' Marvin Bressler, 'The conventional wisdom of education and sociology' in C.H. Page (ed.), *Sociology and Contemporary Education,* New York, Random House, 1964.
21 'Impersonality' is a word used by T.S. Eliot to characterise that feature of the imaginative writer best expressed in Keats's famous remark about 'negative capability': 'that is when a man is capable

of being in uncertainties, mysteries and doubts, without any irritable searching after fact and reason.' In other words, Keats was arguing an objectivity of the poet also. He was to allow the flow of experience to shape itself without too rapid or too overt an interference. A poet is not a propagandist.

22 At stake, of course, are two conceptions of 'nature' — a human nature, in the one case, suffused with value and the need to take moral and value decisions as a defining characteristic of its being, or, in the other, one treated as a 'scientific' object whose behaviour is (at least ostensibly) subjected to impersonal, value-free observation. From the latter in a world where value decisions are inescapable is derived a view of human conduct which imperceptibly comes to take on the characteristics of a norm — illegitimately, because all such investigations can hope to reveal is how men do behave (assuming their accuracy), not how they ought to. At the same time, the suggestions made in this chapter concerning the possible uses of the literary artist to the social investigation do not exhaust the possibilities. Thus, in her admirable study of middle-class values in Soviet fiction (*In Stalin's Time*, Cambridge University Press, 1976), Professor V.S. Dunkam uses Soviet middle-brow fiction to point to crucially important developments in Soviet society in the post-war period.

Chapter 3 Discovery methods

1 J.J. Rousseau, *Emile*, trans. B. Foxley, London, J.M. Dent, 1943, p. 59.
2 Ibid., p. 30.
3 Ibid., p. 90.
4 Ibid., p. 31.
5 Ibid., p. 131.
6 Ibid., p. 140.
7 'Other aspects of child psychology' in R.S. Peters (ed.), *Perspectives on Plowden*, London, Routledge & Kegan Paul, 1969, pp. 49-50.
8 There is an admirable study of recent research on progressive learning theories (including discovery methods) in Dr W. Anthony's essay of that name in G. Bernbaum (ed.), *Schooling in Decline*, London, Macmillan, 1979, 'I have concluded', writes Dr Anthony, 'that progressive methods are *not* generally superior to non-progressive methods for the teaching of reading and English, and that progressive methods are generally *inferior* to non-progressive methods for the teaching of arithmetic' (p. 180). Professor Neville Bennett, too, has published a study of *Teaching Styles and Pupil Progress* (London, Open Books, 1976) which indicates, as its 'central factor ... that a degree of teacher direction is necessary, and that this direction needs to be carefully planned, and the

learning experiences provided need to be clearly sequenced and structured' (p. 162).

Chapter 4 The idea of a liberal education

1 Aristotle's *Politics*, trans. B. Jowett, Oxford University Press, 1905, pp. 300-17.
2 P.H. Hirst, 'Liberal education and the nature of knowledge' in *Knowledge and the Curriculum*, London, Routledge & Kegan Paul, 1974.
3 W. Jaeger, *Aristotle*, Oxford University Press, 1962, Appendix II.
4 T. Lund, *Liberal Education for Free Men*, University of Pennsylvania Press, 1951, p. 28.
5 K. Charlton, *Education in Renaissance England*, London, Routledge & Kegan Paul, 1965, p. 6.
6 Quoted in Charlton, ibid., p. 39.
7 Cf. W.H. Woodward, *Desiderius Erasmus*, Teachers College, Columbia University, 1967, p. 163.
8 W.H. Woodward, *Studies in Education during the Age of the Renaissance (1400-1600)*, Teachers College, Columbia University, 1967, p. 246.
9 In any case, of course, Plato remained a pervasive influence during the Renaissance period — as is manifest in the Florentine Academy of the later fifteenth century and in *The Courtier* by Castiglione.
10 Even in classical times, however, it must not be forgotten that for long periods the educational experience was backward-looking cf. R.R. Bolgar, *The Classical Heritage*, Cambridge University Press, 1973, pp. 20-4.
11 J.H. Newman, *On the Scope and Nature of University Education*, London, J.M. Dent, 1914, p. 145.
12 Reprinted in *The Aims of Education and Other Essays*, London, Williams & Norgate, 1947, pp. 66-92.
13 Ibid., pp. 73-4.
14 Max Lerner (ed.), *The Portable Veblen*, New York, Viking Press, 1948, p. 337.
15 Cf. n.2.

Chapter 5 The arts in education

1 Cf. William Nelson, *Fact or Fiction, The Dilemma of the Renaissance Story-Teller*, Harvard University Press, 1973.
2 Cf. F. Gilot and C. Lake, *Life with Picasso*, Harmondsworth, Penguin, 1966, pp. 68-9.
3 Ibid., p. 69.
4 H. Read, *Education Through Art*, London, Faber & Faber, 1961, p. 112.

5 Susanne K. Langer, *Feeling and Form*, London, Routledge & Kegan Paul, 1953, pp. 401-2.
6 Cf. B. Bettelheim, *The Uses of Enchantment*, Harmondsworth, Penguin, 1978.

Chapter 6 The death of Bazarov

1 Lewis S. Feuer, *The Conflict of Generations*, London, Heinemann, 1970, p. 89.
2 I. Turgenev, *Fathers and Sons*, Everyman edition, J.M. Dent, London, 1962, p. 44.
3 Ibid., p. 33.
4 Ibid., pp. 23-4.
5 Ibid., pp. 266-7.
6 Ibid., p. 240.
7 C.C. Abbott (ed.), *The Correspondence of Gerard Manley Hopkins and Richard Watson Dixon*, Oxford University Press, 1953, p. 139.
8 I. Turgenev, *Fathers and Sons*, op. cit., p. 72.
9 Ibid., p. 74.
10 Ibid., p. 71.
11 In a paper on 'Literature and the social sciences' reprinted here as chapter 2.
12 P. Jacobs and S. Landon, *The New Radicals*, Harmondsworth, Penguin, 1967, p. 14.
13 Lewis S. Feuer, *The Conflict of Generations*, op. cit., p. 153.
14 Ibid.
15 H. Kidd, *The Trouble at L.S.E.*, Oxford University Press, 1969, p. 124.
16 The comment made by T.S. Eliot about Henry James, that 'He had a mind so fine that no idea could violate it.' He continues, in a way which is relevant to the theme of this essay: 'In England ideas run wild and pasture on the emotions, instead of thinking with our feelings (a very different thing) we corrupt our feelings with ideas; we produce the political, the emotional idea, evading sensation and thought.' This is surely what *Fathers and Sons* is all about.

Chapter 7 Equality and education

1 *Democracy and Education*, New York, Macmillan, 1921, p. 47.
2 Cf. R. Nisbet, *The Sociological Tradition*, London, Heinemann Educational Books, 1967, p. 148.
3 Nigel Grant, *Soviet Education*, Harmondsworth, Penguin, 1970, p. 30.
4 Ibid., p. 46.
5 *Times Higher Educational Supplement*, 12 December 1972.
6 J. Dewey, *Democracy and Education*, op. cit., p. 101.

7   Ibid., p. 105.
8   Ibid., p. 143.
9   Ibid., p. 144.
10 The implications of the movement have been very well analysed in their effects on English prose by Professor L.C. Knights in an essay on 'Bacon and the seventeenth-century dissociation of sensibility', reprinted in *Explorations*, London, Chatto & Windus, 1946. There Professor Knights points to the diminution of meaning implicit in Bacon's 'subordinating the emotional and expressive to the descriptive and analytic' and the Royal Society's prescription 'reducing all things as near the mathematical plainness as they can'. Under this regime metaphor comes to be illustrative ornament rather than explorative of the phenomenon under consideration: 'the function of the images [in Bacon's writing] is not to intensify the meaning to make it deeper or richer, but simply to make more effective a meaning that was already fully formed before the application of the illustrative device.' Elizabethan metaphor at its finest (e.g. in Shakespeare) implies overtones, ambiguities which far transcend in meaning the new plainness.
11 J. Dewey, *Art as Experience*, New York, Capricorn Books, 1958, p. 270.
12 J. Dewey, *Democracy*, p. 225.
13 Ibid., p. 281.
14 This may seem to be at odds with what I have said earlier (p. 112) where I have suggested that it is art and literature (the humanist tradition) which is complex and ambiguous and therefore opaque, and science which is 'clear'. In fact this is not the case. Art can, of course, be democratised — and in fact is being so. Cf. Roy Lichtenstein and Andy Warhol at the Tate Gallery — a painting of a Campbell's soup tin is quite unequivocal and demotic. The high culture tradition of complex literature and painting is gradually being destroyed. On the other hand, science, which is basically 'clear' at an elementary level, has far surpassed in complexity Dewey's primitive view of it and has come to seem the paradigm of 'knowledge' and 'understanding' in the scientific-technological era.
15 Educationally, the outward manifestation of this is the common curriculum, a device recommended by some members of the left and positively implemented by a Conservative Secretary of State. Cf. *Dilemmas of the Curriculum*, Martin Robertson, 1980, chapter 3.
16 Personally to the present author.
17 T.S. Eliot, *Notes towards the Definition of Culture*, London, Faber & Faber, 1948, p. 47.
18 Ibid., p. 85.
19 T.S. Eliot, 'Burnt Norton, *Four Quartets*, London, Faber & Faber, 1944.
20 T.S. Eliot, 'East Coker', *Four Quartets*.
21 T.S. Eliot, *Notes*, p. 106.

22 Ibid., p. 105.

23 Ibid., p. 48.

24 The best now being claimed for comprehensive schools is that they have made little difference: 'Comprehensives have had little effect either way both on A level passes and the proportion of young people with A levels. They do seem to have something to do with a decline in passes in certain key subjects' (P. Venning, 'A level absolutes', *Times Educational Supplement*, 18 January 1980). This despite vastly increased resources applied to education during the transition (nearly trebled between 1963 and 1973). There is firm evidence that able working-class children suffer in poor neighbourhood schools (cf. V. Bogdanor, *Standards in Schools*, National Council for Educational Standards, Kay-Shuttleworth Papers in Education, no. 1, no date, p. 9); it is commonly admitted that comprehensives have failed in their social aims; serious worries are now being expressed by the Royal Society concerning science education and by others about modern languages. All this confirms the view I constantly reiterated during the 1960s: 'that at most what we are accomplishing is the replacement of one set of problems by another – and these not necessarily less serious' (*Education in an Industrial Society*, 2nd edn, 1973, p. 1). Rigorous selection is developing in Eastern bloc countries, 'key' schools being set up in China. Cf. also Mrs Auriol Stevens's impressionistic but convincing study *Clever Children in Comprehensive Schools* (Penguin 1980), where clever children are shown to suffer even if the mediocre in some sense benefit.

25 Of course environment plays an important part, but almost certainly not even the major role. But even if it were conceded that human beings were *totally* formed by their environments, there is no reason to assume that this would make much difference to the range of achievement by which we are faced. For one thing, as a matter of historical fact, environments are, educationally speaking, both good (culturally rich, emotionally supportive) and bad (deprived emotionally, culturally impoverished). This must be conceded. Now the hope is, of course, that these inadequate environments can be rapidly improved. In fact, in many cases, this will prove impossible. Families are going to continue to split up, parents are going to continue to neglect their children, husbands and wives to separate and divorce, thus causing those emotional troubles in their offspring which we know to represent a major factor in lack of achievement. Furthermore, other families, even when emotionally supportive, will fail to offer the cultural nourishment necessary for achievement. In the wider environment, impoverished cultural offerings via the mass media will continue to retard mental and emotional development – indeed, it is not unreasonable to assume that the situation will deteriorate rather than improve as high cultural standards are sacrificed in a general cultural mediocritisation. In fact the human situation cannot be

manipulated with anything like the ease with which, in the technological era, we have learnt to control the natural environment; and even if it could, there is no reason to assume that the cultural standards of the manipulators would prove, in any profound sense, to be educative. Why should one assume that control of manipulation would be seized by the educated (the 'philosopher-kings') rather than by commercial interests or dictators on the twentieth-century model? All the evidence goes to show that, in the current situation, *these* are likely to exploit such human manipulation as is possible. But, of course, environmentalists always naively assume that the environment will be adjusted to serve *good* purposes.

Index

For Product Safety Concerns and Information please contact our EU
representative GPSR@taylorandfrancis.com
Taylor & Francis Verlag GmbH, Kaufingerstraße 24, 80331 München, Germany